"Most of the time, the truth is hard ... it comes with the good-natured hur... of Brant Hansen, it is God's gift to ...

> **Kyle Idleman**, senior pastor of Southeast Christian
> Church and author of *Not a Fan* and *Don't Give Up*

"Warning to all humans: Brant's wisdom is stealthy. He writes with such humor and insight, the points he drives home will feel like a ninja ambush. Brant has the rare ability to evoke simultaneous bouts of laughter and moans of conviction. Fresh, provocative, and highly entertaining."

> **Mike Donehey**, lead singer of Tenth Avenue North and
> author of *Finding God's Life for My Will*

"*The Truth about Us* reveals the tyranny of our false self and its heroic delusions. But there's good news. If we trust God enough to walk away from this, we can live in freedom with nothing to hide, nothing to prove, and nothing to lose. Brant's message is entertaining, challenging, and potentially liberating. I needed to read this. (So do you.)"

> **Benjamin C. Warf, MD**, professor of neurosurgery
> at Harvard Medical School

"Humans need a stern talking-to from time to time, but those straight-up, unavoidable truths are easier to take when they're tempered with humor, understanding, and well-lived-in love. In *The Truth about Us*, Brant Hansen does that expertly, as he does on his radio show and in all of his writings, because you know he's not asking us to consider truths about ourselves that he hasn't grappled with himself. And he's so funny that it feels like an intimate talk over fries with a friend, not a lecture."

> **Leslie Gray Streeter**, columnist for the *Palm Beach Post*
> and author of *Black Widow: A Sad-Funny Journey
> through Grief for People Who Normally Avoid Books
> with Words Like "Journey" in the Title*

"*The Truth about Us* is another of Brant's somewhat irreligious expositions on the meaning of the life that we (ought to) have in Jesus. Laced with his characteristically prophetic humor, he graciously gives his readers a much needed Pharisectomy. Thanks, Brant—I needed that!"

Alan Hirsch, founder of 100Movements, Forge, and
Movement Leaders Collective and
author of numerous books

"*The Truth about Us* is *the book* 'for such a time as this.' Who would have imagined that an examination of our sinful, narcissistic condition could be laugh-out-loud funny. But Brant Hansen offers just such a gift—one hilarious, convicting, and effulgent with the gospel. I have never in my life come to the end of two hundred pages *wanting* to be more humble. I will be giving his book to all my friends for Christmas, not only because it's the right thing to do but because they will thank me for it later."

Anne Kennedy, author of *Nailed It: 365 Sarcastic
Devotionals for Angry and Worn-Out People*

"Brilliant and extremely timely. *The Truth about Us* is unflinching, hope-giving, and life-changing. I think it's the most convincing account of human depravity I've ever read. And it's certainly funnier than Calvin."

Barry Cooper, author, speaker, and podcaster

THE TRUTH ABOUT US

The Very Good News
about How Very Bad We Are

BRANT HANSEN

BakerBooks

a division of Baker Publishing Group
Grand Rapids, Michigan

© 2020 by Brant Hansen

Published by Baker Books
a division of Baker Publishing Group
PO Box 6287, Grand Rapids, MI 49516-6287
www.bakerbooks.com

Printed in the United States of America

Library of Congress Cataloging-in-Publication Data
Names: Hansen, Brant, author.
Title: The truth about us : the very good news about how very bad we are / Brant Hansen.
Description: Grand Rapids : Baker Books, a division of Baker Publishing Group, 2020.
Identifiers: LCCN 2019028674 | ISBN 9780801094514 (paperback)
Subjects: LCSH: Theological anthropology—Christianity. | Identity (Psychology)—Religious aspects—Christianity.
Classification: LCC BT701.3 .H364 2020 | DDC 233/.4—dc23
LC record available at https://protect-us.mimecast.com/s/1gnqCOYk8khp3MXnTE gc5p?domain=lccn.loc.gov

The author is represented by the literary agency of The Gates Group.

20   21   22   23   24   25   26   7   6   5   4   3   2   1

To Darin Hansen.
Thank you for always looking out
for your strange little brother.

It is better to live naked in truth than clothed in fantasy.

—Brennan Manning

Contents

1. Dear Everybody   9
2. Wronger Than We Think   21
3. Your Very Own PR Firm—and Why You Should Fire Them   35
4. Aristotle and My Garage Sale   43
5. Follow Your Heart: The Worst Advice Ever   53
6. The Flaw in Our Code   63
7. Mixed Motives   73
8. So Why Are We Like This?   83
9. Hide the Bud Light Towel: Adventures in Guilt   95
10. Let's Freak People Out   107
11. The Worst Wonderful Word   117
12. A Chainsaw at CVS   127
13. Seven Billion Italian Stallions   137
14. A Short Chapter about the Previous Chapter   147
15. How to Get Kicked Out of the Church of Satan   155

16. Even More Good News: The Humble Life Is More
    Fun Anyway   165
17. The Final Chapter: The One Where I Finally Mention
    Kermit   175

    Acknowledgments   189
    Notes   191

ONE

Dear Everybody

An Introduction to Our Biggest Problem

> All have turned away, all have become corrupt;
> there is no one who does good,
> not even one.
>
> —Psalm 14:3

Dear Everybody,

We have a serious problem:
All of us think we're good people.
But Jesus says we're not.

Sincerely,
Brant P. Hansen

PS: The rest of this book is the PS.

IF YOU THINK I'M WRONG—about how we think we're good people—I offer this challenge: Go ahead and ask someone. Seriously, if you're reading this at a coffee shop, ask the stranger sitting at the next table, "So, are you a good person? Would you say you're more moral than the average person?"

Given my studies in this area, I can predict their response with 98 percent confidence, and it's "I'm calling the police." But while the authorities are being dispatched, try to get a serious answer. If they give you their honest take, you'll hear something like, "Why, yes, I do think I'm more moral than the average person."

This is predictable because social scientists have asked these questions for decades, and the result is the same: *We all think we're more moral than average.* It's remarkable how good we are. Just ask us, and we'll tell you about it.

We can fool ourselves about a lot of things. (For instance, I persist in believing I'll be able to eventually dunk a basketball, despite the fact that my vertical jump is decreasing and I'm actually getting shorter.) But of all the things we delude ourselves about, our moral "goodness" is our biggest self-deception.

Researchers at the University of London concluded that "a substantial majority of individuals believe themselves to be morally superior to the average person" and that this illusion of ours is "uniquely strong and prevalent." They write, "Most people strongly believe they are just, virtuous, and moral; yet regard the average person as distinctly less so." And among their study participants, "virtually all individuals irrationally inflated their moral qualities, and the absolute and relative magnitude of this irrationality was greater than that in the other domains of positive self-evaluation."[1]

And we have a lot of self-delusions. Perhaps you've heard that 93 percent of us genuinely believe we're above-average drivers. Perhaps you've seen studies that show we also think we're smarter than average. And we're friendlier too. Plus we're more ambitious than average.

You might think with all of this awesomeness, we might have an ego problem, but good news: we also rate ourselves as more modest than others![2]

So, yes, we're better at everything than everybody, but at least we're humble about it. That's not surprising because we're us, and, you know, we're cool like that. But what about people we assume simply *must* be less moral than us? Murderers, thieves, and the like—surely they'd have a more reasonable assessment, right?

Why, no, actually. The incarcerated population also thinks they're more moral than everyone else. Prisoners find themselves to be kinder than the average person. And more generous.

The professor who conducted the study of prisoners wrote, "The results showcase how potent the self-enhancement motive is. It is very important for people to consider themselves good, valued, and esteemed, no matter what objective circumstances might be."[3]

Our goodness is our biggest self-delusion, and all of us seem to be living with it. It's a delusion we seldom talk about, but Jesus is relentless in addressing it in myriad ways. He publicly blasts upstanding citizens for being clean on the outside but not the inside. He tells stories like those of the prodigal son to illustrate how a seemingly good person can be utterly lost without knowing it. He tells the chief priests that prostitutes will enter the kingdom before they do. He tells an apparently

> **The impression I get from Jesus is that the battle against our own self-righteousness is our biggest battle of all.**

law-keeping "good guy" that no one but God is good. Jesus keeps emphasizing that all of us, without exception, need to repent and repudiate ourselves.

In fact, the impression I get from Jesus is that the battle against our own self-righteousness is our biggest battle of all.

With this in mind, here are a few things to consider as you read this book:

1. **This will be challenging, and possibly strange. But it'll also be fun. It will be strangely fun.**

   The truth about *The Truth about Us* is that it's about *all* of us. You're not being singled out. You don't need to feel guilty for being a human being. And you know what? Learning about how we all operate can be fascinating and even amusing.

   Roughly speaking, that's what the first half of the book is about. Then we'll more fully discuss what we can do—and give up doing—to make a refreshing difference in how we see the world and operate in it.

2. **You'll gain insight into your own behavior and thoughts and into how others work too.**

   This can mean gaining the peace and freedom that comes from growing up, from refusing to play the same tiring mental games our entire lives in order to justify ourselves. The burden gets lighter.

3. **This is written by someone who thinks Jesus is an authority.**

I don't mean just "an authority" either, but The Authority. Jesus is at the center of my view of the world. If you're not a Christian, I think you'll still enjoy this book and even find yourself nodding in agreement at times.

4. **This isn't written textbook-style.**

While I'd like these concepts to be taken seriously, I'll be writing in a conversational style. This is because (a) I tried to make this book all academic-y, but (b) I bored myself into a stupor. So I started over.

5. **We're not only going to talk about the truth about ourselves. We're also going to talk about what to do about it.**

The goal here is not for you to walk away thinking, *Wow, Brant. Now I see how self-righteous I am. Thank you. I feel tingly all over.* No, the goal is to lighten your load, and to help you see just how good God is and how much more relaxing life can be when we come to terms with who we are. The same Jesus who keeps trying to show us how we're not as good as we think we are is the one promising that his way is lighter and easier.

Another goal is to sell twelve million copies of this book, launching a nine-episode film series starring Viggo Mortensen as me. So there are a couple goals here.

Plus *The Truth about Us* action figures. So that's three goals now, I guess.

Anyway, the point is, I hope you read this book and are inspired.

6. **When we discuss "self-righteousness," here's what I mean.**

Biblically, the word *righteous* means approved by God. It's something God judges as good or right. To be self-righteous, then, simply means we've met that standard in our own eyes. As we'll see, this is very, very important to us and, I believe, animates so much of what we actually do in life.

Jesus warns us against our self-righteousness in the most dire terms. (He uses the word *hell* a lot more often than most of us are comfortable with.) He's quite aware that while we humans have seemingly insatiable, unstoppable lusts for everything— fame, money, sex, power, tickets to *Hamilton*, pumpkin-spice products—it's actually our pride that will doom us.

In this book, I'll show you how we will often stop at nothing to avoid cognitive dissonance. We will twist logic, bend reason, conveniently forget facts, invent new stories, even destroy relationships—all in the name of preserving our precious illusion. We'll sacrifice anything. It really is that important to us. This is how addictions work, and when it comes to our own need to be "right," well, we're all addicts who need to be set free.

A warning: It's true that observing how we humans really operate is a little unsettling. But let's also admit it's entertaining too—kind of like that Super Bowl halftime show with the Rolling Stones when Mick Jagger was flapping his arms around. Sure, we were mildly disturbed and we're all still processing it, but we're going to be okay. We went through it together.

The "At Least I Don't . . ." Delusion

Jesus keeps trying, over and over, to get us past our favorite delusion. In Scripture, one of his favorite ways of getting around our defenses is telling brilliant short stories. He uses the following story to put his listeners (and us) on notice: "Good people" often kid themselves.

> To some *who were confident of their own righteousness* and looked down on everyone else, Jesus told this parable: "Two men went up to the temple to pray, one a Pharisee and the other a tax collector. The Pharisee stood by himself and prayed: 'God, I thank you that I am not like other people—robbers, evildoers, adulterers—or even like this tax collector. I fast twice a week and give a tenth of all I get.'
>
> "But the tax collector stood at a distance. He would not even look up to heaven, but beat his breast and said, 'God, have mercy on me, a sinner.'
>
> "I tell you that this man, rather than the other, went home justified before God. For all those who exalt themselves will be humbled, and those who humble themselves will be exalted."
>
> Luke 18:9–14 (italics mine)

The hero of the story is the man who knows he's not a good person. He doesn't equivocate in the least. He offers zero excuses. He compares himself to no one. He doesn't offer an "At least I don't . . . ," as in "At least I don't murder people," or "At least I'm not racist," or "At least I'm not lazy." He refuses to even try to justify himself.

Jesus promises people like that will be lifted up.

Notice what he promises for the outwardly good guy who offers the prayer with "At least I don't . . ." at the heart of it: He's going to be brought down, hard.

I've learned that Jesus is both terribly dangerous and terribly safe. For the proud, he is the biggest threat imaginable. And for the humble, he is the securest refuge.

And then we have Jesus, just a few verses later, nailing the point to our front door, in case we missed it:

> A certain ruler asked him, "Good teacher, what must I do to inherit eternal life?"
>
> "Why do you call me good?" Jesus answered. *"No one is good—except God alone."*
>
> Luke 18:18–19 (italics mine, but I bet Jesus wanted it italicized)

This is very hard for us to accept. "I'm not a good person" is a shockingly countercultural thing to say. We all want to think we're "clean" and that we've avoided whatever "big sins" are on our own personal lists. But we trust ourselves too much. We are inconsistent. We don't even live up to our own stated beliefs. (Just think about all the things you've faulted others for. Have you always lived up to those standards yourself?)

Here's something we perhaps don't think about much that demonstrates that we're truly not good like God is good: *We fail spectacularly to love like he does.* Honestly, do we really love people well? Everyone? Consistently? Or is it truer that we actually fail at this practically every hour of every day?

> I've learned that Jesus is both terribly dangerous and terribly safe. For the proud, he is the biggest threat imaginable. And for the humble, he is the securest refuge.

God is love. He is good. He is the standard. We're good too, if we love like he does. Do we really believe we're anywhere close to that?

While Jesus tells us that no one is good but God, he then does something we still struggle to understand: He demonstrates vividly on a cross that our value doesn't depend on our goodness at all.

The Weirdest Thing to Say

It almost sounds crazy: "Hello. My name is Brant, and I am not a good person."

Not only is it countercultural, it even runs counter to our physiology. Studies show we actually get a dopamine hit when we think we're proven right. We can literally become addicted to the sensation of our rightness. "Your body does not discriminate against pleasure," writes clinical psychologist Renee Carr. "It can become addicted to any activity or substance that consistently produces dopamine."[4]

> We actually get a dopamine hit when we think we're proven right. We can literally become addicted to the sensation of our rightness.

This might explain why we spend time scrolling through and enjoying information and news links that prove—once again—how right we are. Wow, do we love that feeling. It also might explain why many have gone to their graves insisting they were right, even if it made them miserable in the process. Addictions work that way.

W. H. Auden was right: "We'd rather be ruined than changed."[5]

Jesus insists on this willingness to change, because he knows that self-righteousness will separate us from God forever. We're all at high risk of becoming sick with self-righteousness, and if we don't submit to his healing, it's terminal.

Listen to Jesus and it sounds like he's doing an intervention, except instead of a group of people surrounding an unbelieving addict, it's the crowd that needs to get the message, and just one man is delivering it.

"Interventions" like that historically haven't ended well for the message bearer. Calling out our self-righteousness isn't popular, and believe me, this isn't lost on me as I'm writing. (Note to self: Next time, use a pen name. Pick something cooler than "Brant Hansen.")

> FAQ: But, Brant, don't you think that the author of a book on self-righteousness can be self-righteous himself?
>
> A: YES. A thousand times, yes. This is a daily struggle for me.

It so happens I'm dealing with a bit of it right now as I type. Seriously. I'm currently sitting outside a restaurant on a pretty day. A Lexus SUV is to my left, parked in a spot that has a sign in front of it. The sign says that only people with a permit for disabilities can park there. The man who parked there does not have said permit. A lady in the spot next to him called his attention to the sign. He looked at it, shrugged, and walked off. I am morally superior to him.

I like to call this "righteous indignation" because he's clearly wrong, but if I'm being honest, it's not just indignation. It's tastier than that. I kind of enjoy it. There's a sweetness in noticing the flaws in others, and—oh wait, here comes the guy. He's finally leaving. I was hoping he'd get a ticket, but he didn't. It would have felt great to see him get his comeuppance.

I don't park in handicapped spots. Me? I break other laws. Like the speed limit. But at least I don't do the thing that guy just did. (I'm kind of a Jedi master with the "At least I don't . . ." thing.)

So, yes, I'm as self-righteous by nature as you are. Like Steve Brown writes, "It is difficult (maybe impossible) to write about self-righteousness without being self-righteous."[6] I'm not exempting myself from any of this. Imagine this book is like an AA meeting and I'm the guy standing next to you, pouring myself a Styrofoam cup of substandard coffee. There's no finger pointing. This is why the book is called *The Truth about Us* instead of *The Truth about All YOU Guys.*

It's helpful to know what's driving us. And in this book, I want us to consider the possibility that our lives are largely shaped by this desire to convince ourselves that we're good people.

This is what it means to be human and broken. Pull up a folding chair next to me, or maybe next to a thief who is world-renowned for doing nothing impressive whatsoever, except realizing he had done nothing impressive whatsoever. But he admitted the truth about himself and the truth about Jesus: *I'm a sinner, and he's the King.* We know about him because he's the first person—and the only person in recorded history—to whom Jesus says, "Today you will be with me in paradise."

TWO

Wronger Than We Think

Battling Self-Righteousness with an Awareness of Our Self-Wrongness

It is quite possible that I may be altogether wrong in this idea. My own impression, however, is, that I am right.

—Wilkie Collins

We're going to discuss "wrong," but first, let's discuss Brant Hansen–level wrong.

In South Florida several years ago, there was a skywriter who occasionally spelled out happy messages about God—things like "God loves you." Often, on a clear morning, you could step out and see the pilot's handiwork.

One morning, as I started my workday as a morning-show host on a local Christian radio station, I read a news website that reported his death. He'd been killed in a plane crash near the Fort Lauderdale airport.

I made the announcement on the show, and the response was immediate and overwhelming. People jammed the phone lines, crying and recounting one story after another about how the pilot had encouraged them deeply at just the right time. Stuff like, "I was headed to the hospital for more tests one morning, wondering if God even cared, and I looked up in the sky . . ." and "I asked God if he really loved me while I was driving home from my night shift, and I looked up, and . . ."

They were very emotional. It was moving. Yes, it was tragic, but this was also some very compelling radio I was doing.

I leaned into it. I changed some of the songs and played emotional ones. More tears. More people calling. Lines jammed. I hadn't planned on it, but I decided to make my whole show about it. It was amazing radio.

Midway through the morning, I got a call. "This is incredible!" a young guy told me on the air, fighting back tears. "Someone has picked up his mantle, and now *they* are writing 'God loves you' in the sky! This is beautiful!"

Sure enough, more callers.

"He may have died, but his legacy lives on!"

"This is amazing!"

"Wow! I can see it now!"

More emotional music. What a show.

There was only one problem: He wasn't dead.

Turns out it was *him* in the sky, trying to prove that he was still alive, because he couldn't get through on our busy phone lines. He knew his friends and neighbors would be panicking, and he wanted to show he yet lived.

At 5:30 a.m., for an apparently brief time, the website had it wrong. I didn't ever double-check. I didn't know he was alive until my show was over. When my manager told me,

"Hey, I just saw something online, and I think that guy isn't *that* guy," I wanted to teleport to the surface of Saturn.

It all ended well. Sort of. I mean, it ended as well as hosting an entire show about the death of a man who hadn't died can end, I think. I had to do a lot of apologizing to listeners and to the skywriting guy himself. He said it was frustrating but oddly interesting listening to his own funeral on the air. (My new *Brant Hansen Show* motto idea: "Frustrating but Oddly Interesting.")

What We Thought We Knew

Sometimes it's good to be dreadfully, unmistakably, inarguably wrong. I really mean this. It's brutal, but it's very healthy. And by "healthy" I mean, "Wow, it's going to hurt to remember this, but you know what? At least I'll remember it."

> When are five times I've been obviously wrong? Or even three times? Specifically, what are those examples?

Most of the time, we don't remember being wrong. We all think, *Me? I'm wrong a lot. Of course!* But ask yourself, *When are five times I've been obviously wrong? Or even three times? Specifically, what are those examples?*

It's not easy. This is because we tend to screen out our wrongness. We simply can't remember. Kathleen Schulz writes extensively about how difficult it is to be wrong in her aptly titled book *Being Wrong*:

A whole lot of us go through life assuming that we are basically right, basically all the time, about basically everything:

about our political and intellectual convictions, our religious and moral beliefs, our assessment of other people, our memories, our grasp of facts. As absurd as it sounds when we stop to think about it, our steady state seems to be one of unconsciously assuming that we are very close to omniscient.[1]

She tells the story of a particular psychologist who was a kid during World War II. He distinctly remembered exactly where he was when Pearl Harbor was bombed. He was listening to a baseball game when the news of the bombing interrupted. It was a vivid memory to him, and a "Where were you when . . . ?" story he'd told many times over the years.

Until the 1960s. That's when he stopped telling that story. He stopped because it dawned on him: The bombing of Pearl Harbor was on December 7. They don't play baseball in December.

Fascinated by the disconnect between his own absolutely certain memory and reality, he was ready when another "Where were you . . . ?" moment came up. When the space shuttle *Challenger* exploded after takeoff in 1986, he immediately had students write down where they were when they got the news. In their own handwriting, they recorded the details of their story.

Then, a decade later as part of his research, he contacted them and asked them to tell their stories again. The result? "Only 7 percent of the reports matched the initial ones, 50 percent were wrong in two-thirds of their assertions, and 25 percent were wrong in every major detail." One participant said, "I know that's my handwriting, but I couldn't possibly have written that."[2]

Rarely does anyone go to this length to confront us with

ourselves. As a result, we get to walk around convinced we're the ones who remember it right, whatever "it" was.

I've experienced that very strange feeling—I'm not sure what to call it—when I've gone from completely sure of myself to "Wait, what?" It's like a kind of vertigo. Like I'm suddenly free-falling. Here's how it usually happens:

Me: I did not text the guy last week to come over and fix the whatever.

Wife: That is false. You texted the guy last week to come today to fix the whatever.

Me: No. We talked about it, but I did not text him. That's a fact.

Wife: Yes, you did. I was standing right here when you did it.

Me: Okay, then, let me show you my texts, and [looks at texts] . . . Hey, are we having pork chops tonight?

Wife: We never have pork chops. You're just changing the subject to the first thing that popped into your head to create a diver—

Me: Do you like Pac-Man?

Not only do we remember things much less accurately than we think, we're also apt to underestimate our unawareness.

We Don't Know What We Don't Know

Years ago, I watched the classic video on YouTube of a group passing a ball back and forth. It's a pretty simple exercise.

> **Not only do we remember things much less accurately than we think, we're also apt to underestimate our unawareness.**

You're supposed to just count the number of times a group of people pass a ball among themselves as they stand in a circle. ("Sounds thrilling, Brant! Thanks for the entertainment tip! My weekend is SET.")

But there's a fun twist (spoiler alert). After the video, when people have counted the passes, they're asked a question by the group leader: "Did you notice the gorilla?"

As you know, whenever someone in leadership asks the insightful question, "Did you notice the gorilla?" it's worth stopping to reflect.

If you rewind, you'll see that midway through the video, someone dressed in a gorilla costume actually strides into the middle of the circle, beats his chest for a while, and then casually walks away.

The vast majority of people notice exactly zero (0) gorillas in the video. They're too focused on counting ball passes. When you rewatch it and you're looking for a gorilla, you can't miss it. It's absurdly obvious. Dominating, even.

We miss so much, and it's not even because we're looking the other way. We miss things directly in our path, directly in front of us.

In his book *Traffic*, author Tom Vanderbilt talks about research into driver behavior and how oblivious we are to what's actually happening on the road. It's not just that drivers are alarmingly unaware of real hazards, it's that we're completely unaware of how unaware we are. We might narrowly miss a pedestrian and not realize it. Often we only become aware of our limitations, Vanderbilt points out, on those occasions we call "accidents."[3]

We have much to learn. More than we think. No wonder James advises us in the New Testament to "be quick to listen, slow to speak" (James 1:19).

There's another very inspiring verse about our wrongness. It's in Proverbs. It's about how we should humbly approach what little we actually know and how our own judgment can be compromised. Notice how, in a nuanced way, it gently, poetically, and very subtly suggests that we should be amenable to possible course correction: "Whoever hates correction is stupid" (Prov. 12:1).

> We have much to learn. More than we think. No wonder James advises us in the New Testament to "be quick to listen, slow to speak" (James 1:19).

Being unaware of how unaware we are is merely one way to be wrong. It's just one of the many options in our Tool Belt of Wrong. We have common, systematic ways of being wrong, termed *cognitive biases* by cognitive scientists.

So Many Biases

One of the leading people in the field of cognitive science is Daniel Kahneman, who's won a Nobel Prize for his work as a moral psychologist. As we examine his work, this becomes obvious: *We're so beset with inherent biases, we need other people desperately.* We simply can't trust what we see, because we lie to ourselves so often and so easily.

Is there a way to overcome our wrongness on our own? "You won't find anyone more pessimistic than I am," Kahneman told a writer for the *Atlantic* in an article titled "Your

> We need other people who will speak the truth to us, even when we don't want to hear it.

Lying Mind." He argues that we're "hardwired to delude ourselves."[4]

Indeed. We need other people who will speak the truth to us, even when we don't want to hear it.

One well-known cognitive bias is *confirmation bias*. It means that we tend to interpret and remember information that confirms what we already think. Not only that, we actively seek out this kind of information. (Eureka! According to the news channel I agree with, I'm right again!)

Years ago, I bought an iPhone. Whenever debates come up about iPhones versus the alternatives (which are actually more popular), I'm anxious to find information that confirms the superiority of iPhones. Is it because I desperately want Apple to succeed?

No. It's because I want *me* to succeed. I want my decisions to be right. I want to think of myself as a smart person. So I defend my previous decisions, even if I know precious little about the subject.

Confirmation bias is even more powerful when it comes to bigger decisions. I desperately wanted to think I was smart about buying a more expensive car, so I sought out positive reviews after I bought the car. It sure makes me feel better about myself, even if it was a big mistake.

I was engaging in what's called *selection bias*, which we use to try to help convince ourselves of our rightness when we have any lingering doubts. Researchers say when we're less confident in our opinions, we're more likely to seek out only the information that affirms us.

What's more, if we voice our opinions on an issue, if we take a stand, we get even worse about this. Scientists call this *attitude polarization.* Simply put, if we openly, publicly commit to a position, we will entrench ourselves more deeply in that position, even in the face of mounting evidence against us.

Imagine how this applies to social media. The other day, I saw a colleague post something about election laws. He was manifestly, provably wrong. I was embarrassed for him. Unsurprisingly, a commenter quickly responded with, "Hey, man, that's not true. Here's the actual law," and included an authoritative link. Did it matter? You can probably guess the answer to that. Once we take a public stand, it takes an almost shocking amount of humility to back down.

> If we openly, publicly commit to a position, we will entrench ourselves more deeply in that position, even in the face of mounting evidence against us.

And then there's another common bias called *hostile attribution bias* that we all apparently kind of enjoy. It's simply the "tendency to interpret others' behaviors as having hostile intent, even when the behavior is ambiguous or benign."[5]

I get to be on the receiving end of this one quite a bit, thanks to the way I look, which is inappropriately intense. It's part of my apparent lifetime commitment to using all the wrong body language. I have a dark cast. I furrow my brow. I don't make eye contact much. Because of a neurological condition, I shake my head "no" all day long. It's like I'm a precision-designed Horrible First Impression Bot.

On a near daily basis, I have someone asking me what my "problem" is. I offend people without saying a thing.

I'm buying a pack of gum, and the Walgreens lady is put off by the way I'm, you know, existing. "What's the matter with you? You got a problem?"

"No, I just want some minty-fresh gum."

Hostile silence.

Of course, I could be misreading her seemingly angry "You got a problem?" too. Like Kathleen Schulz wrote, we see ourselves as omniscient, but we should admit we don't really know what motivates people.

A perhaps more insidious route to wrongness is the *illusion of control*, a bias that disposes us to put ourselves, once again, directly at the center of our universe.

In one experiment, researchers would equip each participant with a button and put lights in front of them. Participants were told the button may or may not have anything to do with how the lights turned on or off. In some cases, the buttons were actually connected to the lights, but for others, there was no connection at all.

The result? Subjects in both the connected group and the unconnected group thought they were controlling the lights with their buttons. Their confident sense of control was unaffected by whether or not the buttons were connected to the lights.[6] (In related news, it's only been in the last few years that I've begun to suspect those "close door" buttons inside elevators are hooked up to absolutely nothing.)

It's also true that we don't think others are in control like we are in control. When it comes to driving, for instance, we think it's much, much safer if we're driving than if we're in the passenger seat. We think we're far more likely to be hit from behind than we are to hit the car in front of us.

We're wrong about how "in control" of things we are. Again, we see ourselves as a little more godlike than we should.

Scientists call it the *overconfidence effect*. One manifestation of that particular cognitive bias is *overplacement*, which is simply thinking we're better than everybody else at most things. It's that simple. As we already noted, this is famously illustrated in the classic finding that 93 percent of us think we're better-than-average drivers.

> We're wrong about how "in control" of things we are. We see ourselves as a little more godlike than we should.

Kahneman says that we have to struggle to remind ourselves that we are perhaps in the grip of an illusion. We simply aren't as right, or as righteous, as we think we are. (By the way, when I get my first copy of this book, I'm going to underline that last sentence. I might even circle it. I'd recommend you do the same, but I don't want to be Bossy Author Guy.)

There's the *empathy gap* too, wherein we underrate the influence of our own feelings. We think we're driven by our reason. We're wrong.

And there's the *hindsight bias*, a way of tricking ourselves into thinking we "knew it all along" when we really didn't. We're wrong.

Ever wonder why so many prices end in ".99"? Because marketers are aware of *left-digit bias*. If something sells for $1.99, it sounds a whole lot better to us than $2.00. We think we can afford more items if the items end in ".99." We're wrong.

A favorite of mine is the *third-person effect*. We're prone to think mass media has a big impact on people—but not us, of course. Other people. And we're all familiar with the *bandwagon effect*, a proven bias that leads us to believe something if everyone else seems to believe it, even if it's tragically wrong.

You get the idea. There are more than a hundred recognized cognitive biases, and so many of them are rooted in our desire to divide the world into the "Good People" and the "Bad People" and see ourselves as one of the former. We engage in little shortcuts, so many ways of fooling ourselves, and we're largely blissfully unaware.

We want to think we're good, or another person is good, based on a relative standard. But God doesn't look at the outward appearance. He looks at something we can't see: the heart (see 1 Sam. 16:7). As we'll discuss later, even seemingly "Good People" are beset with motivations that fall far short of the standard of God's goodness. We're all capable of doing wonderful things, but if we're being perfectly honest, our motives remain a mystery even to ourselves (see 1 Cor. 4:1–5).

"The heart is deceitful above all things," the Lord famously says in Jeremiah. "Who can understand it?" (Jer. 17:9).

So let's admit it: We're biased. We don't see things clearly all the time. In fact, we can't objectively see what's driving us, or anyone else, at all. We can't pretend we're good when we don't even know our own motives. We can be wrong about a lot of things.

Where does this leave us? It sounds like we can't definitively say where anyone else stands with God. It sounds like we can no longer confidently divide the world into the Good People versus the Bad People. And sure enough, it sounds like the proper response to God is exactly what Jesus was saying it should be, exactly like what the tax collector cried out in Jesus' story.

"Have mercy on me, a sinner."

THREE

Your Very Own PR Firm— and Why You Should Fire Them

Battling Self-Righteousness by Stopping the Spin

> I never made a mistake in my life; at least, never one that I couldn't explain away afterwards.
>
> —Rudyard Kipling

And this, of course, brings us to what is my favorite social-scientific experiment involving pantyhose.

Researchers in the 1970s (which, not coincidentally, is when people last used the word *pantyhose*) stood outside a fancy department store and asked women passersby to check out samples of four different pantyhose brands. They'd then ask, "Which one do you like the most?"

The subjects' opinions varied widely from each other, but they were very decisive. "This one is clearly better," or "This one is much softer," or "This one is such higher quality."

As it turns out, they were all the exact same pantyhose. So let's pause here to note (1) we will come up with an opinion whenever we're asked for one, and (2) "Professors Pulling Pantyhose Pranks" is an excellent name for a punk band.

But what happened next is the really bizarre thing. When told that the samples were, in fact, all the same, the subjects doubled down! They felt a need to defend their stated opinions, even in the face of the seemingly indisputable. They tried to argue that the researchers were wrong.[1]

We don't know why we do some things or say some things or feel a certain way. But we'll come up with reasons anyway, and we'll talk ourselves into it.

We find ourselves very persuasive. Immediately.

It's not just *what* we're capable of rationalizing that's remarkable, it's *how quickly* we start doing it. Even with little things, petty likes and dislikes, we get the machinery working fast. *Bam*. It's that quick. I don't have a hard-and-fast opinion on whether Iowa or Nebraska is the better state, but if you force me to have a preference, you can bet I'll be marshaling every argument at my disposal to prove why my brand-spanking-new opinion is 100 percent right.

> Once I hear myself giving my reasons, I find me terribly convincing.

And once I hear myself giving my reasons, I find me terribly convincing. We all have the remarkable ability to go from no opinion to strident in seconds.

What's more, even when we *know* what we're saying is wrong—when we *know* we're lying—we begin to believe ourselves! Researchers at the University of California, Davis, demonstrated this using magnetic brain imaging. People volunteered—and I, for one, thank them for this—to spend blocks of time in an fMRI tube. Then researchers asked them, "How enjoyable was that?" (Spoiler alert: It turns out it was not at all fun, which confirms my personal policy of not volunteering for tasks that involve the words "my head" and "in a tube.")

The researchers asked a group of the subjects to lie about the experience and say they enjoyed it. They had the subjects fill out evaluations, telling them that upcoming patients would be calmed by reading positive reviews. So the volunteers claimed they actually enjoyed being in an fMRI tube, all the while knowing that they weren't telling the truth.

In follow-up interviews weeks later, those subjects who left misleading reviews actually claimed that they *did* enjoy being in an fMRI tube. They really had a good time after all! Turns out it was quite pleasurable, this tube.

How does this happen? We can actually persuade ourselves to believe alternate versions of reality when those versions help us think better of ourselves. We don't want to think, *I'm lying*, because that might make us feel guilty, and we can't stand to perceive ourselves as liars. So we have cognitive dissonance, and we try to get rid of it. We'll reshape reality to preserve our self-perception.

Dissonance theory predicts that we will eventually (and conveniently) forget good arguments made by opponents just as we forget silly arguments we made ourselves. . . . *It's motivated by our need to be right*, preserve self-esteem . . . and gradually come to believe in our own lies.

Here's the thing: No one is immune to the need to reduce dissonance, even those who know the theory inside and out. In reality, we're all suckers for a happy ending, even if it's one that we have to make up for ourselves or even piece together with tape.[2]

Exactly. We need to become more aware of how we think, because our thought processes are skewed. Our reasoning is a tool, and it's not the precise, calculating, impartial tool we like to think it is. Every waking moment, it's put to work to defend us and our conception of our good selves.

We Are Excuse Machines

"Our in-house press secretary automatically justifies everything," writes the brilliant social psychologist Jonathan Haidt. "If you want to see post-hoc reasoning in action, just watch the press secretary of a president or a prime minister take questions from reporters."[3]

No matter how ridiculous any given decision by any given administration is, an articulate someone will trot out to defend it. It's an exhausting and thankless job, but we all sign up for it on our own behalf. We have to be in defend-and-convince-ourselves mode 24/7.

Just like in politics, we can offer some ridiculous excuses. Some of my favorite examples are from sports, like in the World Series, when legendary pitcher Roger Clemens actually picked up a piece of a bat and threw it at a base runner he'd had a previous incident with. He said it was all an accident, because—in spite of a lifetime of experience—he confused a bat with a ball. (Note to Roger: You're not supposed to throw the ball at runners either, but whatever.)

A pro cyclist was busted for banned-substance use after he won a race in Germany. He said it wasn't his fault. He'd ingested the stimulant on accident because he ate too much of his father-in-law's pigeon pie, and the pie was made from racing pigeons that had been drugged. (Wait, people eat pigeon pies?)

Here's a personal favorite of mine: North Korea lost in the Women's World Cup in 2011, and the coach said there was a good reason. After all, the players were tired after an earlier practice match, when each and every one had been struck by lightning.

I work in radio, and I've mastered this excuse thing. I've done it with ratings. Before the ratings even come in, I'm all set: If they show me in first, it's because I worked really hard. If I'm in last, well, that's because ratings are dumb. Plus the sample size is too small. And that other station is giving away a car. I can't compete with that. The other station has thirty-seven people on their zany "morning zoo" show. How can I compete with a thirty-seven-person zany morning zoo team? I DON'T EVEN KNOW HOW TO BE A ZANY ZOO.

What a waste of time. If I clear this protect-my-rightness narrative from my agenda, maybe I'll have more energy and brain space for other things. Important things. Like writing books with sentence fragments. Like this one.

We really can be free. We don't have to do this excuse making. We don't have to employ a full-time, internal PR spokesperson. We don't have to defend ourselves against the truth about us.

"Come to me, all you who are weary and burdened, and I will give you rest," Jesus says (Matt. 11:28). Perhaps that rest involves being able to stop all this machinery in its tracks. By admitting how we can fool ourselves, by admitting we're addicted to our own rightness, by rethinking how we approach life, we may just also find this oft-elusive "peace" he spoke of.

No more justifying, no more constant rationalization. This is the beauty of actually saying, "I am not a good person."

I can even laugh at myself when, say, the pantyhose experimenter people tell me it was all a ruse. And I don't actually have to cherry-pick the Bible for Scriptures to justify my current beliefs or past actions, because now I'm free to learn with less of my ego to protect.

It makes me less of a jerk. It makes me less judgmental of others. Once I stop feeling like I need to defend my goodness and rightness, I'm more patient with myself. That helps me be patient with others too.

> No more justifying, no more constant rationalization. This is the beauty of actually saying, "I am not a good person."

For much of my life I've had a scoreboard mentality, like there's a cosmic point system, and it shows how I'm doing and whether God should be mad at me or reward me. I've extended that mentality to others. Should I be mad at them or reward them? Are they deserving of my approval? It's another big, dumb, tiring, waste-of-time process.

When we accept the reality of our own propensity to be wrong, we might be more patient with ourselves and gentler with others. We'd begin to see them through a new, more merciful lens.

Mercy is a wonderful time and energy saver too. When it comes to humanity, there's plenty to judge, for sure, but do you really want that job?

No, You Don't Want That Job

A friend of mine named T (seriously, that's his name) says something really weird happened to him once, right after he got married. He heard God say something. Or he thinks he did, anyway. The content of the short message smacked him in the face, he told me.

"So my wife and I were having a big argument about something, and I was totally right," he said. "You know how most of the time you might be right or you're both kind of right, or something, but this time—totally seriously—I was absolutely right, and I knew it, and it was incredibly frustrating. I was so angry. She was absolutely being wrong."

So what happened?

"I went in our bedroom and I was seething. And that's when something popped in my head, and it practically knocked me over. I honestly think it was something God was telling me directly. Totally stopped me in my tracks."

And what was that?

"It was, 'So, do you want me to judge her right now?'"

Whoa.

"Yes. Honestly, I'd never even thought about that sort of thing. It was completely out of the blue, and it made me feel sick. I knew immediately that the answer was no, of course. I love my wife. I don't want God's judgment poured out on her, or me."

I thanked him for the story. He told me this a few weeks ago, but I've thought about it a lot. Interestingly, T is a lawyer and has a skeptical mind. I could tell it still shook him to think about it. It shakes me a bit too.

I think about all this sometimes, and even though I'm not a particularly emotional person, I get so deeply thankful, I can feel it. I'm so glad for this thing called grace. I just can't keep track of all this good-person/bad-person business.

I don't want to fool myself anymore with my own self-saving narratives. I don't want to decide when and how others should be judged. I don't have the time or energy. I don't want to be like Adam and Eve, using my imagination to try to cover my shame with fig leaves.

> I don't want to decide when and how others should be judged. I don't have the time or energy.

Sometimes I think about how singular, and how shocking, grace truly is. I'm not the smartest guy in the world, but I know a good deal when I see it.

I'm taking this one.

FOUR

Aristotle and My Garage Sale

Battling Self-Righteousness with Servanthood

> Have you ever noticed that anybody driving slower than you is an idiot, and anyone going faster than you is a maniac?
>
> —George Carlin

Regrettably, we've come this far in our little book about human behavior without mentioning IKEA.

But the streak ends now, because there's a fun cognitive bias called the *IKEA effect*. It holds that we value something more if we had a hand in building it. We might even overvalue it. I might sell you this well-built dresser for $200, but this other one—you know, the one I sloppily assembled with an Allen wrench while trying not to cuss?—well, that one will cost you $400.

Researchers cite the success of Build-A-Bear stores to illustrate how the IKEA effect works. I can vouch for this. My daughter has chucked 98 percent of her childhood stuffed animals, but there is one that remains: Blaze the Pony. Many years ago, she pressed a button and then watched as a limp pocket of furry fabric filled with stuffing and became a little horse. She *made* Blaze.

There's nothing wrong with valuing something more if we made it, of course, but this is another example of how we are all dealing with subtle biases that might throw off our judgment. I consider Blaze the Pony priceless too. After all, she's my daughter's pony. Hard to believe, but I don't value your daughter's stuffed pony quite as highly.

This is related to the *endowment effect*, which is pretty simple: Things that remind me of me are more valuable. Stuff gains value just by being associated with me.

Things that remind me of me are more valuable. Stuff gains value just by being associated with me.

Richard Thaler, a University of Chicago economist and Nobel Prize winner, conducted research about this phenomenon. In one famous experiment, he and his research partners divided a group in two, and each member of one group was shown a mug and asked how much they would pay for it. The average answer? $2.21.

Members of the other group were each given a mug and then asked how much they'd sell it for. The average? $5.78.

As soon as a mug becomes My Mug, it gains value. Why? If I was just given the mug, it's not like I have fond memories of it. It has no sentimental value, except that I'm a bit sentimental about me. It's worth more now because it's My Mug, not Your Mug.[1]

Researchers have studied this in many ways and reached the same conclusion. One study gave each member of one group a chocolate bar and each member of a second group a mug. (And before you ask, no, I have no idea why they keep using mugs in these studies. Cognitive scientists, can we branch out and maybe do some cups? Goblets? Steins?) They asked the chocolate bar people if they'd like to trade for a mug. They said no way. They would not trade their chocolate bars for mugs.

Next, they asked the mug people if they would trade for a chocolate bar. No, they would not trade their mugs for chocolate bars.[2]

How is this possible? Again, the endowment effect is in play. Once something is associated with me, once it's mine, it's worth more. I'm good, so it's good. Losing it is a little threatening. I take it personally. It makes a kind of sense, once we admit that we put ourselves at the center of our star systems. Mugs—and really, all drinkware—in our orbit are more valuable.

Even Aristotle noted this in his nutty-fun lecture series, *The Nicomachean Ethics, book IX*: "Most things are differently valued by those who have them and by those who wish to get them: what belongs to us, and what we give away, always seems very precious to us."[3]

But honestly, I already knew this, and I'll bet you did too, so I really didn't need Aristotle for this point. I'm just quoting him because it's cool to quote Aristotle.

I became aware of the endowment effect when a crowd of people very recently brutalized my sense of self-worth.

They systematically looked through an array of my belongings I had attractively set before them, then rendered their bitter verdicts.

Out loud. To my face.

It was an event we hosted called a garage sale, and in it I vulnerably offered my electric football game—a classic American game wherein you put little plastic guys on a small metal "field" and then plug it in, and it vibrates and everyone runs in circles. That game is easily worth $55.

The crowd rejected this appraisal. They found it to be worth—and this hurts to type—75 cents.

> Did they see the value in my Lord of the Rings Pez dispenser set? No, they did not.

They did this with every awesome thing I owned. Did they see the value in my Lord of the Rings Pez dispenser set? No, they did not. I explained the storytelling genius of J. R. R. Tolkien, his masterful layering of myth, and his love for linguistics. I showed them how I would use the Pez dispensers on my desk to reenact the battle of Helm's Deep.

They firmly rejected me. Not the Pez dispensers. Me.

The endowment effect explains much, including why I still have my Lord of the Rings Pez dispenser set. We think something's more important because it's ours, even when our wives want us to get rid of it. (There needs to be a value study for married people. In my own home, many objects I value at $50 and above are valued by my wife at approximately "Set it on fire.")

Not only that, but we like things to be devalued, at least a bit, when they cease being associated with us. An example: Researchers at the University of Western Ontario studied how people "creep" on their exes online following a breakup. "We're hardwired to pay attention to other people," they said, which sounds pretty nice of us . . . until the researchers explain why we're paying attention: "Even if we broke something off, we want to fundamentally believe that no one can replace us. *We want affirmation that we're valued or a good person*, so we're hoping that without us they're going to be a little bit sad or suffer a little bit."[4]

There's even a theory called the *name-letter effect* that holds that we like certain letters more than others. The ones we like most? *Our initials.* What's more, it's so powerful that we're attracted to people who have similar names to ours.[5]

It's not just letters and Pez dispensers that gain value when they're associated with us. We do the same thing with people. We tend to favor strangers who have a certain "look." We just trust them more. We implicitly grant them extra credit for being good people if they have this look. And that look is . . . like us.[6]

So I trust people who look like Brant Hansen, or at least people I think look like Brant Hansen. You know, guys like Hugh Jackman. He's trustworthy to me.

We assume that if someone looks like us, they likely act like us, and *we* are certainly trustworthy. As we know well by now, we see ourselves as the standard bearer.

It's not just driving, as the quote at the beginning of the chapter reminds us. It's everything.

I don't think about food much. But when I occasionally pass on some waffle fries, people call me a health nut. I'm clearly *insane*. I've taken leave of my senses.

That said, if someone exercises more than I do, well, I suspect they're spending too much time focusing on their bodies. Kinda shallow, you know? And if they exercise less, I think they're ignoring an important part of life.

So what's the right amount of exercise? However much exercise Brant Hansen does.

There. That settles it.

People drink too much when they drink more than I do. They're taking sports too seriously when they take it more seriously than I do. They're playing music too loud when it's louder than I'd play it. They're looking at their phone too much when it's more than I look at my phone. They're not concerned enough about the environment if they're less concerned than I am. And let's face it, if they care more than me, they're environmentalist wackos.

> So many wackos in the world. Why can't they just do the right thing and be like me?

So many wackos in the world. Why can't they just do the right thing and be like me, Brant Hansen?

Seventeen Cats in My Living Room

Once, I had an epiphany. And, like most epiphanies throughout history, it happened while watching the TV show *Hoarders*. If you haven't seen the show, it's about what you'd expect: people who collect things, or refuse to throw away things, and wind up living in absurd, chaotic, messy homes.

I enjoyed it until I realized one reason why I enjoyed it: because these people affirmed my goodness.

Now, I may be a mess—but I'm not *that* bad. My living room may be a total disaster, but at least I don't have forty-six cats living in it. I only have seventeen. That person is exactly twenty-nine cats worse than me. Who keeps forty-six cats in a living room? Freaks, that's who.

Yes, my garage is an epic mess, but at least it's not filled with 890 jars of old buttons. I've got my quirks, but I'm no 890 Jars of Buttons Guy, I'll tell you that right now.

This seems to be what drives much of our entertainment programming. Daily talk shows are deliberately populated with people who are an obvious disaster, because programmers know it draws us like an accident scene.

We may be materialistic, sure, but at least we're not as shallow as the Kardashians. We may be mean and gossipy, but we're way better than *The Real Housewives of Wherever*. I may lie a little bit, but not like those people on *Survivor*. I may not be the best parent, but I'm better than that Honey Boo Boo mom lady or whatever that show was. What a weirdo *that* lady was.

I type all these things knowing full well these references will date this book. For all I know, these shows aren't still in production. I've never watched them. (See? I'm not like those people who watch shows like that. I'm a good person.)

Each freak show–style program reinforces our natural desire to see ourselves as the norm, the standard. So, yes, we can laud ourselves for having ethical standards. It's just that our standards so often are ourselves.

Just ask two recent presidents of the United States, one from each party. One said he believes in God but doesn't need to ask him for forgiveness.[7] Another says he believes in God too. He acknowledged that he sins, but for him, "sin" is when he's out of alignment with his *own* values.[8]

I don't mean to pick on politicians. That's too easy. I think these people represent all of us. In significant ways,

> It's not a matter of merely *staying* humble, because humble is not our default. This is a mind-set we have to cultivate.

we really are profoundly, deeply biased toward ourselves. This is why it takes continuing intervention, continuing re-newing of the heart and mind, or we slip into making ourselves the standard for all things that matter. We have to ac-tively humble ourselves, Scripture says. "Humble yourselves in the sight of the Lord, and He will lift you up" (James 4:10 NKJV).

And it's not a matter of merely *staying* humble, because humble is not our default. This is a mind-set we have to cultivate.

When Jesus tells me he is the teacher and we are all the students (see Matt. 23:10), he's giving me a reality check. I am not The Standard by which good and evil are judged. I don't get to grade everybody's papers. If I want to think otherwise, he says, well, I will be humbled (see Matt. 23:12).

It's taken me a long time to understand this, but I think I finally get it, thanks to the IKEA effect: When Jesus tells me to love my neighbor and even to love my enemies, and to "do good to those who hate you, bless those who curse you" (Luke 6:27–28), he's doing me a favor. He knows if I assume the posture of a servant and humble myself, I will see reality more clearly. I will invest others with value when I pour myself into them. That's literally what it means to *bless*—to add value to someone. I will regard them as more and more valuable as I actively serve them.

My obedience changes my heart.

Popsicle Guy

Jesus demonstrated humble servanthood a thousand ways, of course, but one very vivid way was through washing the feet of his own followers. Honestly, I wish it weren't so. I hate feet. My own feet, other people's feet—everybody's feet. I hate them. It even creeps me out to type the words "other people's feet."

But a couple times in my life, I've been politely guilted into "foot-washing" ceremonies, wherein groups of people gather around and take turns getting on their knees with a bucket and sponge and washing each other's feet.

One of those ceremonies happened in Costa Rica. It was hot and humid, and at the end of the day, people in my travel group were pretty smelly. We didn't have air-conditioning. Our only cooling-off break during the day was when a small, middle-aged guy came around pushing his popsicle cart.

At the end of a very long, very warm day, our group leader announced we were going to do a foot-washing ceremony as a part of our evening worship service. When it was my turn, they handed me the towel and sponge, and I got down to wash the feet of the next person who sat down, which was . . . the Popsicle Guy? I didn't even know he was mixed in with the group.

As I knelt, grabbed his dirty, bare foot, and started washing, something happened: I started feeling an intense concern for him. For his wife. For his kids. For his hopes and dreams. For everything he wanted in life. I wondered where he came from. What was his story? What were his parents like?

I moved to his other foot. I thought about what an honor it was that I was now crossing paths with him. I asked God

> Even if you're not "feeling it"—even if you're not motivated to wash feet, for example—there's something about investing yourself anyway that will shape your heart.

to bless him wildly. Suddenly I found myself caring about a man I'd barely noticed.

There's something freeing about this. Even if you're not "feeling it"—even if you're not motivated to wash feet, for example—there's something about investing yourself anyway that will shape your heart. It can be as simple as praying for people. I've never been a good prayer, and sometimes I don't know how to serve particular people. But Jesus tells us to even pray for our persecutors, and I find I'm more prone to be *for* people as soon as I've prayed for them.

The endowment effect is real. It's a great way to look at the price of mugs, but it's an even better way to see how we thrive by moving past our damaging obsession with ourselves.

Popsicle Guy wasn't just Popsicle Guy anymore. But he didn't change. I did.

FIVE

Follow Your Heart: The Worst Advice Ever

Battling Self-Righteousness by Challenging Our Own Thinking

> i had a long talk. with my fren. about how to spot. a fake ball throw. the optimal strategy. is to follow the ball. with your eyes. instead of your heart.
>
> —Thoughts of Dog (@dog_feelings)[1]

Once you start paying attention, you can't help but notice how good we all are at this rationalizing thing.

Me? I consider myself the LeBron James of rationalizing. You can't stop me. You can only hope to contain me. I will drive the Lane of Rationalization with impunity, dunk directly in the Face of Actual Reality, and then complain that I was fouled by the Power Forward of Unfairness.

53

My ambition to do all this is perhaps matched only by my desire to stretch NBA metaphors.

You may not be the LeBron of rationalizing, but you might be the Kobe. Because everybody's got a gift for this.

"The talent for self-justification is surely the finest flower of human evolution, the greatest achievement of the human brain," writes Michael Foley in his bestselling book *The Age of Absurdity*. "When it comes to justifying actions, every human being acquires the intelligence of an Einstein, the imagination of a Shakespeare, and the subtlety of a Jesuit."[2]

Here's how it works: I like to think I'm a rational guy. I like to think I dispassionately line up reasons, and when my rational mind tells me something is logical to believe, I believe it. I then act on those beliefs and have to bring my emotions into line with cold, stark reason. Because, like I said, I like to think I'm rational.

Problem: None of this is actually true. It's a fantasy world. *None of us actually works this way.*

Jonathan Haidt, in his book *The Righteous Mind*, likens the way we actually work to an elephant and a rider. We like to think the elephant is our reasoning, and the rider—our emotional or intuitive side—is just along for the ride. But everything in Haidt's career as a social psychologist shows the exact opposite.[3]

> Our rationality is not in charge at all. We're kidding ourselves.

Our rationality is not in charge at all. We're kidding ourselves. Our rationality is the rider. The elephant goes where it wants. Our emotions and intuitions lead us. Instead of being guided by reason, we just employ reason to come up with justifications for why we should believe what we already wanted to believe. We line up our reasons to fit what we already want.

And wow, are we good at it. I shudder to think how many times I've done this. For example:

> Me (walking in a mall): I'm on a very strict bud-
> get. No way can I afford a shirt right now.
> Even if it's on sale. It's not happening. Nope.
>
> New shirt: Check me out. I'm on sale. And I'm
> cool. I have the little shoulder-button things
> you like.
>
> Me the next day: Hey, everybody, check out my
> new shirt with cool shoulder-button things.

Now, if you heard the entire internal dialogue, you'd be witness to genius: "Okay, yes, I'm on a budget . . . but that's an awesome shirt. And 40 percent off is a big sale. You don't see that every day. Perhaps I needn't be so hard-and-fast with the 'budget' idea, given that, say, my utility bill might be lower than expected this month. And since I *will* need more clothes at some point, it would be irresponsible to wait until I need a shirt and then have to pay full price. So, if anything, I'm actually acting out of fiscal responsibility by buying this shirt. I'm saving now so I don't have to pay full price later.

"I simply must conclude that it would be irresponsible to *not* buy this shirt with the shoulder-button things. Positively reckless. And I am *not* a reckless person with my finances. I want to be responsible. Ergo, I am totally buying this awesome shirt."

Done deal. I've used my reasoning to back up what I wanted to do. That's how we operate.

Or there's always this familiar scenario:

Me: I resolve that I will eat super healthy this
week.

Chips: Here we are. We came with the sandwich you
ordered.

Me: With malnutrition so widespread, what kind
of person would I be to let you go to waste,
chips? What kind of humanitarian would do
that? I simply am obligated to eat you, chips.
Thank you, chips.

And voilà, I've convinced myself to eat chips, with the
bonus of being a true citizen of the world.

To avoid embarrassment, I'm using benign examples, but
please know I've certainly enlisted my power of reasoning
for more serious matters too. Like Haidt says, the elephant
wants what it wants, and I, the rider, creatively line up reasons why it all makes perfect sense.

The One I'm Fooling Is Me

Notice that in the above examples, none of the dialogue
was said out loud. That's because when we rationalize, it's
not primarily to convince others. It's to convince ourselves.

Guy Swanson writes about why a person would do this in
his book *Ego Defenses and the Legitimization of Behavior*:
"He must deal with the impulse in such a way that he rein-
states himself in his own eyes. Without that reinstatement,
he is divided against himself and he therefore has difficulty
in functioning."[4]

It's all about using our own brains to fool ourselves. Swanson says that we fool ourselves so we can place our desires in a context that makes fulfilling them justifiable. That way we can still believe our "essential goodness of character."[5]

> We want what we want, and our reasoning is given an assignment: Make it okay.

We desperately want to be a good person in our own eyes, and we will rearrange everything to make it happen. We want what we want, and our reasoning is given an assignment: Make it okay.

We'll even start not knowing things we once knew. Whatever it takes.

Last week a friend of mine called, upset. A friend of his, a married father and devout Christian, told him he's no longer convinced of the claims of Jesus. Over the last few weeks, he had begun to question everything. Suddenly he found long-discredited arguments to have a certain validity. Perhaps the Gospels were written hundreds of years after Jesus? Perhaps Jesus was married and had kids? Perhaps . . . ?

Recalling previous experiences with this sort of thing, I asked, "Just curious: Did he mention anything about his love life?"

Why, yes, as it turns out. He'd fallen in love with another woman a couple months ago.

There's nothing unique about this gentleman. He's a human, and this is the sort of thing we do. Yes, he's torpedoing his family. Yes, he's in the process of causing immense hurt and decades of regret. But he still wants to be a "good person," and that's causing dissonance, so something has to go. In this case, it's his faith.

Yes, our reasons naturally follow our wants, not the other way around. Life would be easier were it not so.

You might ask, "Wait, if this guy is so intelligent, so well-read, so reflective, why can't he see this himself? Isn't he well aware of the damage he's doing? He's crushing his wife and children. He knows better. He's aware of the ethics of that."

Of course he is. But intelligence and education don't help us overcome our self-righteous ego defenses. In fact, they can hurt. This sounds counterintuitive, though certainly I fancy myself a highly rational person who's (of course) more intelligent than average. That's why I really hated reading about a study that indicated intelligent people are *more* prone to fool themselves, not less.

The study, conducted by researcher David Perkins, asked people of varying ages and backgrounds to examine a contentious social issue and list reasons for their personal opinions. He also asked them to list reasons for the other side. He found that people with higher IQs were more proficient at coming up with reasons . . . but only for their own side. They showed no enhanced ability to see things from another person's point of view.

Perkins says people "invest their IQ in buttressing their own case rather than exploring the entire issue more fully and evenhandedly."[6] Smart people are simply more adept at lining up reasons for what they already believe. In a very real way, smart people are more adept at being wrong.

Break Out the Mordor Memes

When I see "Follow your heart" on social media, it usually appears over a beautiful photo of a beach sunset. If the meme makers wanted to be more accurate, they wouldn't show a beach. They'd give us the Cracks of Doom. This is because "Follow your heart!" or "Trust yourself!" may be the worst advice in the history of advice.

These sayings sound like ancient wisdom, but they're not. Quite the opposite, actually. For example, Proverbs 21:2 says, "A person may think their own ways are right, but the Lord weighs the heart."

And then there's "The way of fools seems right to them, but the wise listen to advice." That's in Proverbs 12:15.

A resounding warning about our ability to rationalize comes from Proverbs 16:2: "All a person's ways seem pure to them, but motives are weighed by the Lord."

There's the decidedly unsubtle message of Proverbs 14:12: "There is a way that appears to be right, but in the end it leads to death."

And just in case we didn't fully absorb that one, Proverbs says the exact same thing a couple chapters later: "There is a way that appears to be right, but in the end it leads to death" (16:25).

Okay. Got it, Proverbs writers. Sheesh.

It's worth noting that these verses were written a very, very long time ago. This is a consistent human problem. (New slogan: "Humans: Pulling the Wool over Our Own Eyes for More than 2,500 Years.")

> New slogan: "Humans: Pulling the Wool over Our Own Eyes for More than 2,500 Years."

Obviously, as we already know, when Jesus was tackling people's self-righteous delusions, he was attacking a problem that had been around a while. If we want to understand human behavior, we have to understand both our desire to think of ourselves as good and our willingness to jump whatever hurdles necessary to do it.

One of my favorite ways to avoid acknowledging reality is this little move—and I've actually said this: "I'm sorry I did that. It just wasn't me . . ."

Yeah. "It just wasn't me." Maybe you've heard that before.

But if it wasn't me, it sure looked like me. Messy brown hair, about 5'10", perpetually confused look, scruffy beard. Fits the description. He even carries my driver's license.

But I know I'm a good guy, and since good guys don't do that thing I just did, that couldn't have been the "real" me. The "real" me is right and moral and upstanding. The "real" me is not the guy who just did something selfish.

"That wasn't me . . ." No, that *was* me. The real me. Just as "me" as the guy who helped the old lady across the street.

We have to recognize we're self-righteous by default, and that means constantly correcting our imaginary view of ourselves. And wow, are we humans imaginative. For example: In 2017, three of the remaining leaders from Cambodia's Khmer Rouge faced trial for their crimes dating back to the 1970s. What did they do? They enslaved and executed their own people, resulting in 1.5 million deaths of the innocent. Women, children—everyone.

After all that time to think about what they'd done, exactly zero (0) of them were sorry. They claimed they were completely justified in what they did. When they faced the tribunal, they still regarded themselves "in a morally righteous light." They supervised the mass deaths of the innocent people of Cambodia because they were "defenders of Cambodian independence."[7]

But enough about that. Let's lighten things up. Let's talk about Ivan the Terrible. He was a Russian czar who lived in the sixteenth century, and in addition to being, you know, terrible, he was amazingly theologically astute. He knew the Bible well. He argued convincingly and at length for a biblical basis to his horrifying, murderous reign over his own people. An article in the *New York Times* discussed the ongoing theological debates he had with opponents, and how he utterly dominated them with his biblical knowledge, intellect, style, and panache:

> Ivan's personality shows itself on every page. There is a sort of Shakespearean quality in him. He is passionate and witty, sincere and hypocritical, erudite and totally idiosyncratic; in short, he is extremely individualistic (no wonder, since he was the only human being in his empire allowed to be an individual). His speech is a magnificent dramatic performance.[8]

That's right. You didn't want to get in a Bible debate with Ivan the Terrible. He knew Scripture thoroughly, and he also tortured and killed hundreds of thousands of his own people in indescribably horrific ways. He made it all synthesize. How could someone possibly do this? Well, he was a very smart man, capable of gymnastic rationalizations. In his fertile, astute mind, he made it work.

("Ivan the Terrible." You'd think his nickname would have tipped him off: "Hmmm . . . I was hoping for 'Magic Ivan.' Maybe I need to reevaluate my approach." But no.)

"Ah yes," you say, "there are evil people in the world, but Brant, you're using extreme examples. I am *not* Ivan the Terrible. I've never, not even once, taken over Russia and tortured thousands."

And while this is probably true (I don't know what you do in your personal life), I want to demonstrate the elasticity of the human mind's excuse-making machine. I want to show what we're capable of when it suits our purposes and to demonstrate the rationalizing mechanisms we use to protect ourselves from the truth about us. The most obvious evils suddenly become somehow murky. The most hideous, blatant truths suddenly become debatable. The most hurtful, selfish acts have to be defended.

I may not be world-renowned Brant the Terrible—pending reviews of this book—but I'm kidding myself if I think this isn't how my brain works.

This skepticism about our own nature jibes *precisely* with how the Bible describes us. Again and again, we're told not to trust our own judgment, not to lean on our own understanding. We're warned repeatedly about the deceptiveness of the human heart. And, of course, as noted, we're told repeatedly that none of us are righteous.

Remember the prelude to the story Jesus tells about the self-deluded Pharisee and the humble tax collector? It says the audience for the story was a group that "trusted in themselves that they were righteous" (Luke 18:9 NKJV). Jesus is giving us a beautiful alternative: Don't trust in yourself that you're righteous.

You don't have to. He's done the work.

All your work, all those mental and emotional contortions, all that implausible fleecing for yourself—you don't have to do any of it anymore. You can stand up, raise your right hand, and say, "I'm not a good person. Lord, have mercy on me." And you know what? He will.

SIX

The Flaw in Our Code

Battling Self-Righteousness by Acknowledging the Human Condition

> The depravity of man is at once the most empirically verifiable reality, but at the same time the most intellectually resisted fact.
>
> —Malcolm Muggeridge

Entertainment Weekly asked Jonathan Nolan, one of the creators of *Westworld*, why the show seemed so negative about human nature. "Many times this season," the reporter wrote, "we're told the human race is broken—that we're selfish creatures, intent on our own destruction, incapable of truly evolving and learning from our past mistakes."[1]

So, why not more optimism about human nature? Nolan's answer is blunt.

It's a [bleep] total disaster. . . . I've been reading a lot of history this season, a little bit connected to the show, but also just following the train of things I'm interested in, and it's depressing to realize how familiar some of these problems are, right? It's like we just can't figure these [bleep] things out. We come back to them again and again. It's as if there's a flaw . . . in our code and it follows us around.

Wherever we go, there we are. And we just can't get out of our own [bleep] way. All the beauty and incredible things we brought, and we just consistently find a way to [mess] it up. . . .

At a certain point you gotta [bleep] call it. We're not going to fix this. . . . But there does seem to be a pattern of behavior that follows us, that history echoes from the past, the same mistakes, the same foibles.

So you say: At what point does this fix itself? Or are we just stuck this way?[2]

Yes, it's as if there's a "flaw in our code," indeed.

This is not a popular message. Rarely does anyone voice it. We don't want to hear this. Some things are just not said often in public.

But Nolan is merely echoing a view of humanity that's been common throughout history, and for good reason: Yes, we are capable of astonishing beauty and breathtaking sacrifice, but wow, are we ever messed up. Nolan's show is holding out hope, not that God will rescue us or ultimately set things right, but that robots will get it right, since humans clearly won't.

Most people, of course, have a much more positive view of human nature than *Westworld*. Studies show Christians and non-Christians alike think humans, by and large, are good.

One study found that about two-thirds of us think that, sure, we all might sin a little, but we're mostly good by nature.[3]

Of course, as we've already seen, we all think we're better than average. But we also think the average is pretty good. We think we just have to tweak some things and we're all set.

It's really a wonderful vision of the world, and if it weren't for one minor detail—all of human history—it would be totally believable.

The Times, They Aren't A-Changin'

The other day I saw a comment on Facebook: "It's sad to see what humans have become." It was in response to a news story that was triggering indignation that particular day, about a young girl who had set up a lemonade stand, only to have it closed down by local authorities. They said she didn't have a permit and that she couldn't block the sidewalk.

What humans have *become*?

First, Alexander mass-murders his way from Macedonia to Afghanistan. Then, hundreds of years later, Genghis Khan does the same, going the opposite direction. And now? *A lemonade stand has been unfairly shut down.*

What we have become?

I know it's easy to take potshots at dumb Facebook comments. I've written my share. But it's a common thing, this state of perpetual shock at the state of humanity. (I wrote about this at length in *Unoffendable*.) We're continually in disbelief. We're dumbstruck. Over and over again. Ad infinitum.

We just can't believe humans do what humans are always doing and have always done.

As soon as we invent something or find something, we seem to figure out ways to exploit or kill people with it. Some of the oldest cave art in the world features—guess what!—humans attacking each other.[4]

Prehistory is littered with evidence of massacres and conflict. War and murder predate nation-states, agriculture, and private property. In the Bible, Adam and Eve have two boys, and one kills the other in a self-righteous fit. Spears and arrows likely hadn't been invented yet, but no matter. We can always find a rock or something.

We call it "inhumanity" when we observe people being cruel and brutal to each other. But really it's just humanity.

Are we getting "better," though? Again, we want to think so, but the news isn't great. In the last century, about sixty-two million *civilians* were killed in wars. You can add another forty-million-plus soldiers. Historians say that out of the past 3,500 years, we've been at war for 3,182 of them.[5]

> We just can't believe humans do what humans are always doing and have always done.

We humans are at war pretty much all the time, and we always have been. The Institute for Economics and Peace recently reported that of the 162 nations they cover, exactly 11 were not currently involved in an armed conflict of some sort.[6]

Even outside the context of war, the news is grim. Think about the many genocides in the last century. The brutal regimes of the Soviet Union's Josef Stalin and China's Mao Zedong resulted in the deaths of more than forty million people at the hands of their own governments. While in Rwanda recently, I visited their genocide museum, which tells the story of how, in 1994, in just a few months seemingly ordinary people turned on their neighbors with a vengeance. The death toll was more than a million.

Yes, it's like there's a flaw in our code. Or maybe it's a bug. A big, obvious one. Perhaps we should admit it.

The word *sin* is unpopular, and honestly, I can understand why. *Sin* has been employed for centuries to control and abuse. *Sin* has been misused to advance agendas of power. *Sin* has been used to burden people with crushing shame . . . which, frankly, is exactly what we might expect sinful humans to do. Anything that can be used as a club—we'll find a way to do it.

We can ignore the word or we can substitute it with something else, but there it is. Whatever we want to call it, it is ugly and on the loose, and we all know it's out there.

But the key for all of us is to realize it's not *just* out there. It's in here too. This is what Jesus keeps pointing to, over and over and over. But we're so beset with the flaw that we struggle to see he's really talking about *us*.

"But Brant, it's not like Jesus said that humans in general are evil or anything."

You might want to sit down.

He actually did say we're evil. He takes it as a given, even. When he's talking about prayer, for instance, he tells people that God is a loving father who won't give his child a stone when the child asks for bread. Of course he wouldn't do that! I mean, he's good. Not like us. We're *evil*. "If you, then, though you are evil, know how to give good gifts to your children, how much more will

> "It's not like Jesus said that humans in general are evil or anything." You might want to sit down.

your Father in heaven give good gifts to those who ask him!" (Matt. 7:11).

Yeah, he actually said that.

When I was explaining to someone what I was writing this book about, and how we like to kid ourselves that we're good people, she agreed. Sort of. "You're right, because compared to Jesus, we're not good," she said.

But that doesn't quite catch it. Jesus isn't saying, "I'm perfect, and you guys aren't quiiiiite there yet," or even, "You guys are solid citizens, but I'm looking for top-notch, EX-CELLENT citizens." He tells us we're evil. He just throws it out there too, seemingly casually.

I wonder if anyone nearby said, "Yeah! Exactly! And . . . wait, what?"

Though you are evil. It's a given.

Like it or not, Jesus isn't saying I have to join the Klan to be evil. I just have to keep on, you know, being what I am by nature, which is all about me.

We Keep Proving Jesus Right

Of course, there's plenty of debate about this "humans are naturally sinful" thing. One of the most influential people in Western culture to challenge the idea is Jean-Jacques Rousseau. I'll spare you the full biography, but he's a fascinating study.

Put very simply, Rousseau believed humans are naturally innocent and that we're only corrupted by civilization. We're naturally compassionate toward others. Rousseau had many ideas about children, whom he thought could be made morally perfect. They need to largely be left alone by adults, and typical educations sap them of their inherent compassion and generosity. Rousseau felt that adults should trust the inherent goodness of their children.

Now, if I was a Rousseau fan and you'd done even a little studying of Rousseau's actual life, we might have an awkward conversation at this point.

You: Didn't Rousseau pretty much treat everybody like dirt?

Me: Well, maybe, but the point is he realized we're all inherently good.

You: So why did he routinely humiliate the mother of his children in public? For years?

Me: Nobody's perfect. I mean, he didn't say he was the most virtuous person on the planet.

You: Actually, he did say he was the most virtuous person on the planet.

Me: Okay, good point. Still, he had some great observations on the natural goodness of children.

You: He didn't actually seem to know any children.

Me: Ha! That's not true! He had five children of his own!

You: He forced his girlfriend to abandon them. Each one. One at a time. As babies. All five.

Me: Okay, still, he was a good guy.

You: No, he was the opposite of a "good guy." People at the time said he was insufferable. Diderot, for instance, said he was "deceitful, vain, ungrateful and full of malice." Grimm called him "monstrous."

Me: Okay, I guess you can interpret that negatively if you like.

You: Voltaire called him a "monster of vanity."

Me: Well, okay, but . . .

You: David Hume also used the term *monster* for the way he treated people. The woman he said he loved said, at the end of her life, that he was a "madman."[7]

Me: How about those Sixers?

The man who is so influential to this day in convincing people we're all inherently good led a miserable, self-centered life. Rousseau and I have much in common, even besides the fact that he's a dead white guy and I plan to be one of those eventually: He had a flaw in his code.

If anyone is qualified to make the case that humans are ultimately good, ultimately compassionate, it wouldn't be a pathological narcissist. It would be Jesus, a man who lived a life of sacrifice, healing, and radical other-centeredness.

But the man who lived that life says we're not good at all. And human history agrees with him.

The Truth Is We Are Flawed and Loved

FAQ #153: Gee, thanks, Brant. This has been a real pep talk. Apparently, humans don't do anything selfless. We never do anything beautiful. It's all negative. We're worthless. You should totally be on the motivational speaking circuit.

A: That's not really a Frequently Asked Question. In fact, that's not even a question.

FAQ: That's a good point.

A: Also not an FAQ. But thank you. And the chapter's not over. There's more to say about this.

The biblical story is about a God who creates a world that is truly good. He pronounces it so at every step. The world is shot through with beauty, micro and macro, that transcends my ability to even discuss it. I only have so many words at my disposal and so much space in a simple book.

But I'm thankful for a Jesus who is so clearly not pie-in-the-sky. His appraisal of our need for humility seems squarely in touch with our current predicament. And the very Jesus who so clearly calls out our bent toward selfishness, who so clearly gives us the bad news about our rampant self-righteousness, is the same Jesus who dies for us. This is the biblical story.

> The more righteous we think we are, the more we diminish who God is, and the more we minimize what he's done for us.

And you know what denial of our flaw does? It keeps us from being able to love God fully. We don't appreciate him as much. We're not as blown away as we should be.

The more righteous we think we are, the more we diminish who God is, and the more we minimize what he's done for us.

After all, if we're all pretty good . . . what was the cross all about? It was all too bloody, too violent. It was muscle and bone and sinew, and once you think about us being generally good people, did we really need all that?

But if the *Westworld* guy is right, that we're profoundly messed up and broken, well . . . thank you, Lord, for loving us anyway. Thank you for offering us supernatural love. We need it. We can't handle this ourselves; we've proven it over and over. We need your love to make this thing work.

The more I embrace that truth, the more astonishing God's love is. "Amazing love, how can it be?" goes an old hymn.

The weight of our brokenness could be crushing, but the Good News really is good: This King, the true ruler, still wants us in his kingdom. And that kingdom is the very thing we're all yearning for. It's the world restored and set right.

Humans are capable of both unspeakable cruelty and unfathomable kindness. I've seen hints of both in my own heart. We shouldn't deny any facet of our existence. We don't have to have a simplistic "We're all good by nature!" naivete or a "We're worthless!" negativism.

Yes, we are all sinners. And yes, there are saints among us. But as Thomas Merton wrote, "A saint is not someone who is good but who experiences the goodness of God."[8]

In Jesus, we see the reality of our condition and the reality of our value: Even as we were mocking and executing him, he loved us.

SEVEN

Mixed Motives

Battling Self-Righteousness by Admitting What We Don't Know

> An obsession with righteousness (leading invariably to self-righteousness) is the normal human condition.
>
> —Jonathan Haidt

"Isn't it unfair for Jesus to lump *everyone* in as 'not good'?" you may ask. "Surely there are better neighbors than others. Surely there are good citizens. Surely we can be 'good people' if we don't mug anyone or rob banks or go around killing people. Take me, for instance. I don't mug people at all. Not even a little bit. How can I be just as 'bad' as someone who does it all the time?"

You ask fair questions. You are perceptive. That's just one of the things I love about you, in addition to your sophisticated taste in books.

"Yes," I respond. "Sure, some people behave in more neighborly ways than others. Some people are clearly better citizens. Some people are easier to live with, especially if they don't tend to break into my house or punch me in the face."

I don't say it out loud, but I suspect a village of me's would be a very low-crime place. A village full of Brants would have no street crime. No graffiti. Very few pawn shop robberies. There would be some jaywalking, yes. And everyone would be pedestrians because Brants can't fix cars, so there's that. But it would still be a nice place for Brants to live, right? We could leave the doors unlocked.

But I'm not so sure I can congratulate myself for such good citizenship. Should we really be convinced that our outward, mostly law-abiding goodness is indicative of who we really are inside? Isn't human behavior more complex than that?

Take my "selfless acts," for instance. I've given my money, time, and effort—in addition to risking my life—to help children with disabilities all over the world as an advocate for CURE International. (Impressive, no?) It's also true that, at another level, I rather like it when people are impressed by the fact that I help children all over the world. (Not so impressive, no?) And I like adventure too. I like going to exotic, strange, or dangerous places. It's fun for me.

There's actually an entire website called Humanitarians of Tinder, featuring profile photos from the dating app. People posing with poor children here, with special needs children there, all using the photos (and, presumably, the kids as props) to attract romantic interest. Did some of the people serve because they cared for others? Probably, but here we are again, hoping someone notices.

Mixed motives is an apt way to describe practically everything we do. We might keep all the societal rules, but it might not indicate internal purity at all. Even the most seemingly selfless acts may be from an amalgam of hidden intentions, some flat-out selfish. After all, good behavior earns treats.

Religious Evildoers

Here's where I need to bring up something Jesus said that's highly unsettling. I almost don't want to talk about it. But there it is in Matthew 7. It likely blindsided the people listening. He said there will be people who seem perfectly good who will get some mind-blowing news on judgment day: "Many will say to me on that day, 'Lord, Lord, did we not prophesy in your name and in your name drive out demons and in your name perform many miracles?'" (v. 22).

These people will say, "Lord, Lord . . ." That means they are theologically correct about Jesus. They believe the right things. They emphasize that they know Jesus is the authority.

These people will say they did impressive things—real things, good things, even miraculous things, and in Jesus' name, no less. And Jesus won't argue with them. Apparently, they really did those things.

These people certainly seem like good people.

Then there's Jesus' response to these good, upstanding citizens: "I never knew you. Away from me, you evildoers!" (v. 23).

"Evildoers"? Jesus doesn't even say, "Away from me, well-intentioned people who kinda got off track!"

Again, shocking. They were doing *good* things.

This knocks us off-kilter so much that we almost don't know what to do with it. We like to think if we do impressive good stuff, we get some leverage on God. We obligate him to say, "Nice work. You were one of the good guys," and then give us a reward.

But according to Jesus, there are no good people, only humble people and proud people. He favors the humble and opposes the proud.

Please consider this for a moment: We are all about being good people. But in so many different ways, both Jesus and the Bible are saying that God isn't looking for moral impressiveness. He's looking for humility.

While this is all very disruptive and disorienting—is there anything else in the world that works like that?—I've come to realize it's a breath of fresh air. After all, if indeed we are a mixed bag of motives, how can we ever be sure of where we stand? How can we parse whether we're acting out of deep moral goodness or some level of selfishness? Even altruistic acts are tempered (or perhaps prompted) by selfish motives. Like Paul writes in his first letter to the church at Corinth, we can't sort this one out:

> I care very little if I am judged by you or by any human court; indeed, I do not even judge myself. My conscience is clear, but that does not make me innocent. It is the Lord who judges me. Therefore judge nothing before the appointed time; wait until the Lord comes. He will bring to light what is hidden in darkness and will expose the motives of the heart. At that time each will receive their praise from God. (1 Cor. 4:3–5)

76

Paul is saying there are "motives of the heart"—our own hearts—that we're not aware of. If you're like me, this just seems right, because we humans are so complex.

There but for the Grace of God

Here's another reason I should refrain from any hint of pride in my "good citizen" self-conception: Circumstances matter.

There's a famous experiment that makes this point beautifully. In the early 1970s, researchers John Darley and Daniel Batson asked a group of theology students to make presentations. In order to make their speeches, each student would need to report to one building and then walk to a second one. In between the buildings, an actor would lie slumped along the path, clearly either drunk or injured. He would groan and cough as each unwitting participant approached.

The researchers wanted to see who would stop and help. There were a few variables: The topic for some of the presenters was (fittingly) the story of the good Samaritan, about passersby and their willingness to help someone in need. Other participants had been instructed to speak on an unrelated topic. Some of the presenters identified as more religious, some less so. Some of them were in a hurry after being told they were running late for their presentation. Others believed they had more time.

The result? Some stopped to help. Some didn't. The biggest factor in determining who helped wasn't their reported religiosity. It wasn't the topic either. (You might think the people who were to speak on the good Samaritan would be more apt to help, but . . . no.) The decisive factor was simply a matter of circumstances—who was in a hurry. The students who thought they were running late were much less likely to help.[1]

Would the helpers have still helped if they, instead of the others, were told they were late? Would the seemingly cold-hearted have still been coldhearted if they'd been the ones with more time? Seems doubtful it would work like that.

Yes, circumstances matter. When it comes to little things, that's perhaps even more obvious. This is why marketers are so concerned with behavior-changing detail. There's an entire industry devoted to curating the music playlists we hear while we shop. Researchers say just one change—say, moving candy away from the checkout aisle at the grocery store—dramatically changes our behavior. It alters how much we spend and what we wind up eating. Yes, I can pat myself on the back for not eating a Kit Kat bar, but it sure makes it easier if I never see one in the first place.[2]

In more serious matters (watch and marvel at how I transition from Kit Kat bars to Nazis), we can look at what happened in Germany in the 1930s and 1940s and be shocked by the people who were complicit or silent in the face of evil. But do we *know* we would have been different? The same us, placed in a different time, place, and culture; raised by different parents; and under different pressures and propaganda . . .

Are we so sure?

I know it's cliché to bring up Hitler, and I could pick hundreds of different historical settings for the same point, but there's a reason I'm choosing this one. I recently read about the trial of Adolf Eichmann, a high-ranking Nazi who was taken from South America to Israel for trial in 1960. Timothy Keller writes about what happened when one of the

survivors of the death camps, Yahiel De-Nur, saw Eichmann
and collapsed to the ground, weeping:

> Sometime later De-Nur was interviewed by Mike Wallace
> on *60 Minutes*. Wallace showed De-Nur the tape of him
> falling down and asked him why it happened. Was he over-
> whelmed by painful memories? Or with hatred? Is that why
> he collapsed? De-Nur said no—and then said something
> that probably shocked Wallace and should shock almost all
> secular Western people. He said that he was overcome by the
> realizations that Eichmann was not some demon but was an
> ordinary human being. "I was afraid about myself. . . . I saw
> that I am capable to do this . . . exactly like he."[3]

Keller's point is that while we all want to say the Nazis
were subhuman, they were just like us. It wasn't just a few
people who carried out the Holocaust. It was a large, highly
educated, highly scientific, highly sophisticated, cultured
population. In the words of philosopher Hannah Arendt,
"The most horrifying things about the Nazis was not that
they were so deviant but that they were terrifyingly normal."[4]

I get it. There's a shock of recognition when we can see
ourselves in those we once thought were monsters. Recently
I met a man in prison who was about to be released after
thirty years. He'd been in prison since he was a teenager. He
was insightful and easy to talk to. He was about my age.

It might be obvious who the good citizen is, right? I mean,
one of us is a convicted murderer. The other one of us works
for a global, charitable hospital network. But God does
not judge based on the outward appearance. He looks at
the heart. One of us grew up in nearly impossibly violent,

abusive circumstances. The other didn't. I needn't pat myself on the back for that.

I'm not arguing that we shouldn't be held responsible for our actions. I'm merely showing how wonderful the God of the Bible is. He's the one who doesn't let us play these hairsplitting games. He's the one leveling the moral playing field, saying we don't think like he does and can't know the things he knows. He's the one telling us to refrain from condemning others, because we don't know what motivates them or us.

He's right. (Of course.) And not only should we refrain from condemning others because of all the unknowns, but we should stop doing it because thinking we're morally superior to other people blinds us. We can't see anything clearly.

Jesus says this condition is like having a plank in our eye. We can't operate this way. Imagine the audacity it would take for an eye surgeon to try to diagnose something and then perform surgery, all while blindfolded.

Think about it: *It's our self-righteousness that keeps us from really seeing people as they are.* People become a means rather than an end. We use them for comparison as we try to assuage our unspoken, even unconscious, doubts that we can ever be good enough for God. "Compassion can never coexist with judgment," observed Henri Nouwen, "because judgment creates the distance, the distinction, which prevents us from really being with the other."[5]

> It's our self-righteousness that keeps us from really seeing people as they are.

Sure, that guy over there may have a speck in his eye, but according to Jesus, it's not something we need to concern ourselves with until our own massive issue is resolved. Our self-righteous state makes us useless.

Paul writes that we should consider others better than ourselves (see Phil. 2:3), but it's tough to do that when we consider ourselves better than others.

The moral comparison game is just so complicated. So many circumstantial variables. Too many unknowns. So many mixed motives. We fool ourselves too much. Being considered a "good citizen" proves nothing about the status of my heart.

I'm not sure what judgment day will look like exactly, but if I start with "Lord, Lord, didn't I do that impressive Christian thing? Didn't I travel the world for kids with disabilities? Didn't I go to Christian rock concerts of bands I didn't even like? Didn't I refuse to sing the dirty parts of Prince songs on the radio? Didn't I . . . ," you have my permission to smack me.

"Have mercy on me, a sinner," said the tax collector in Jesus' story (Luke 18:13). The man wasn't a good citizen, and he knew it. But Jesus made him the hero of the story, because Jesus wants us to change. He knows we can. This kind of freeing humility is possible, after all!

"Remember me when you come into your kingdom," said the thief being executed next to Jesus (Luke 23:42). He wasn't a good citizen, and he knew it. But Jesus told him he would be with him in paradise.

I'd like to add a quote here from the woman who crashed a party to throw herself at Jesus' feet, but we don't have one. She wasn't a good citizen, and she knew it—we know that. But Jesus turned to her and said, "Your faith has saved you; go in peace" (Luke 7:50).

We don't even know what she said. The Bible only says that she was crying.

EIGHT

So Why Are We Like This?

> Our souls were made to be blessed and cannot survive without the blessing.
>
> —Dallas Willard

We arrive at a question, and it's important: *Why* do we all struggle with self-righteousness so much?

Put differently, why do we feel such a strong need to convince ourselves we're "good"? And why are we so threatened if someone so much as implies we're not a good person? What's really going on?

When I read the stories about Jesus in the Gospels, he strikes me as someone who is, yes, very frustrated with our condition, but he's also rooting for us. He wants us to get it. He's direct, to be sure, but even when he's arguing with religious leaders who refuse to understand the obvious, he's still holding open the door for them.

He walked through the towns, speaking in synagogues, debating with leaders, and healing the sick. It was one messy, mottled mass of humans after another, the whole lot of them sinners and frustrating hypocrites and self-deluded prideful people. But "when he saw the crowds, he had compassion on them, because they were harassed and helpless, like sheep without a shepherd" (Matt. 9:36).

> We're astray, and we're all looking for something. So what are we looking for?

He looks at self-righteous, delusional us and loves us. We're like sheep to him. We're just plain lost. We're astray, and we're all looking for something.

So what are we looking for?

I have a theory. I would name it "The Hansen Theory of Human Behavior," except I totally stole it from Dallas Willard. Willard was a philosophy professor at USC and is one of my favorite thinkers. He's quoted in John Ortberg's book *Soul Keeping*, giving a possible explanation of what drives us all. I put this quote at the beginning of the chapter, but I'm going to include it again for easy reference. (I'm a full-service author.) "Our souls were made to be blessed and cannot survive without the blessing."[1]

Honestly, I've always kind of recoiled from the word *blessing*. It struck me as a grandma thing to say, and possibly religious sounding to the point of being meaningless in conversation. "Be blessed!" or "Blessings!" or "Bless your heart!"—please know these are all things I'm too cool to say.

But the word *blessing* in the Hebrew of the Old Testament means specific things: It means to bow before someone. It means to honor them. It means to treat them as something valuable.

In their book *The Blessing*, John Trent and Gary Smalley make the point that the Hebrew word for *bless* captures a word picture, that of adding valuable coins to a scale. So when I'm blessing someone, I'm adding value to them.[2]

This kind of blessing is a big deal. In the Bible, for example, the early patriarchs, Abraham, Isaac, and Jacob, offered specific prayers for and prophecies over their children and grandchildren. There's a famous scene where Jacob steals his father's formal blessing from his brother, Esau. Esau is crushed. The blessing meant that much.

Trent and Smalley explain that a formal blessing always contained these elements: meaningful and appropriate touch, a spoken message, and the picturing of a special future of the one being blessed. It also included "an active commitment to fulfill the blessing."[3] It's simply about attaching high value to the one being blessed.

The Party I Never Saw Coming

Last Saturday night, my wife, Carolyn, and I went to a girl's birthday party. At least we thought it was a birthday party. But once we arrived, we thought, *Wait. This isn't just any birthday party.*

The first tip-off? The giant throne.

Seriously. Front and center in a very fancy hotel ballroom. I did not expect this. We know the family, and they are not wealthy. And yet the place was clearly set for an elaborate, expensive banquet.

We were seated, and a formal ceremony began. It was all in Spanish, and I don't know any Spanish. I am passably fluent in one (1) language, so I had no idea what was going on.

There were singers. There were speakers. Everyone was dressed to the hilt. And then processional music began as teenagers, dressed in tuxes and elegant gowns, walked through the room. They gathered in their places around the throne. That's when the birthday girl arrived.

We all turned and followed her as she slowly walked from the rear of the room to the front. The music grew in intensity, and her court gathered in lines for a ceremonial Guatemalan dance before holding palm fronds overhead to form a walkway to her throne.

When she sat down, we all sat. Her father, my friend Elias, began to speak in Spanish. A young man jumped up to offer an English translation. I was grateful.

The girl's parents each put their hands on her and prayed a blessing over her. Little children brought out a succession of gifts: A pair of shoes. Jewelry. A crown.

Elias bent down in front of his daughter and put the sparkly shoes—high heels—on her feet. She'd never worn high heels before. "You have always been my little girl," he said, "but today I recognize you as a woman." He spoke of her intelligence and grace and her kind heart.

Her parents draped her with jewelry while praying over her, then placed a crown on her head. In front of all of her friends and classmates and their whole community, she was praised. Her family and others prayed for her future. Her mom and dad told her how happy they were to be her parents and how they would always be there for her.

I'd never seen anything like this. I'm a Midwesterner, and we tend to want to make sure no one gets "too big for their britches," so I inwardly balked at the whole thing. *Seriously, a throne? I know she's a humble girl, but this is a great way to make someone self-centered and give her a big head* . . .

But then I noticed the boys in tuxes around her. I started thinking about what it must be like to be one of the young men in her court. She's clearly the Special One, the girl of immense value, to her parents and the whole community. Would I treat her differently if I had been one of those young men wanting to be her suitor? Of course I would. This girl—this young woman—was highly regarded, valued, and cherished by all. She was someone worthy of great respect.

The event was five hours. (If you're familiar with a quinceañera, a ceremony for a fifteenth birthday rooted in Hispanic culture, I'm sure you're nodding during this whole description, thinking, *Duh, Brant . . . you didn't know how this works?*)

The whole thing had to cost an immense amount of money. There were clearly months of preparations just for learning the traditional dances. It was the party of a lifetime. Joyful, prayerful, and honoring to one clearly special woman.

My wife talked about it afterward: Imagine the confidence it must give this young woman, knowing she was worth all of that, hearing her wonderful character attributes extolled in public by her mom and dad. How much would it help to hear people who so clearly believe in you gathered around you, praying for a specific, beautiful future?

Now that was a *blessing*. A very formal, painstakingly planned, breathtakingly memorable blessing of a young woman.

We're All Made for This

I think Willard is right: Our souls need blessings. Our souls can't survive without them.

Deep down, we're all aching to know that we're significant, that we're valued, and that our future is secure. Such is the need that Trent and Smalley argue that if we don't get this from our parents—if they don't bless us—it will change the trajectory of our lives. We'll try to find the blessing one way or another—some way to verify that we're significant, valued, and secure.

> Our souls need blessings. Our souls can't survive without them.

This makes sense. The biblical story of humanity begins with us living in the daily, obvious reality of the blessing of God. In the beginning, in the garden, we knew who we were. We knew who we belonged to. We were secure. We were valued. We didn't need to wonder whether we really mattered. We didn't need to justify ourselves.

But we decided to opt for pride over humility, then hide and cover ourselves with excuses. We've been scattered, wandering souls ever since.

I believe we have a self-righteousness problem because of our disaffection from the blessing God offers. We rebel against it. We wind up turning away the very thing we're all looking for. We struggle to believe it. We even simply forget about it.

God has shown us our value through Jesus and promised us a glorious, secure future with him. He has told us we don't need to be anxious and that he will provide for us. He has adopted us into his family. We are infinitely valued as his children.

If I trust him in these things, I will be less, not more, self-righteous. I won't be threatened so easily. My goodness isn't at issue. I will respond and obey my Father out of thankfulness and confidence.

If I don't trust him, however, I will try to find the blessing somewhere else. I will "bless" myself if I have to, and declare my own goodness and value in as many ways as I can.

We've talked about the strange means we employ to preserve our belief that we're good people. Yes, these tactics we employ are a lot of work. Yes, they're tiring. Yes, they're even often delusional. But we do it because we feel like we have to. We need a blessing, even if it's from ourselves. I hope you'll see how, if we begin to understand God's blessing over us, we can be freed from so much of this. There's simply no longer any need to defend our supposed goodness.

And Then There's Cursing

In Scripture, cursing is the exact opposite of blessing. We choose one or the other. "I have set before you life and death, blessings and curses," says the Lord in the book of Deuteronomy. "Now choose life, so that you and your children may live" (30:19).

Now, when I hear a reference to cursing, I think about a list of words my mom is uncomfortable with. But Dallas Willard emphasizes that true curses can be much more subtle and much more destructive.

While a blessing adds value to someone, a curse subtracts it. And boy, do we feel it when we're cursed. It can be the slightest thing. An eye roll. Dismissive body language. An ignored email. Even a slight pause can be a curse, Willard said. A husband can curse his wife with the merest hesitation before saying, "I love you too."

Not only are curses not confined to a list of cuss words, but you can actually curse people by saying completely benign-sounding grandma phrases. We all know "Bless her heart" often means "She's an idiot."

We are so acutely aware of curses. We feel them deeply.

Like the other day, when a guy in a truck honked at me for not running over an old lady. I was taking too long to turn right into a local business parking lot. I was hesitating because the lady was walking across the drive. Being a humanitarian and generally in favor of old ladies, I opted not to hit her with my Volkswagen. But Angry Truck Guy judged me anyway. He apparently didn't see the lady, so he drove away thinking I'm a bad driver who just wanted to slow him down. It irked me and took me a few minutes to let it go. Don't judge me, man.

So unfair.

He was subtracting value from me and my character and my driving skills. By nature, I am very sensitive to feeling even slightly judged, and I'm not alone. This isn't scientific or anything, but I'm pretty sure 90 percent of nonpolitical Facebook rants are of the "don't judge me" variety, followed by reassuring comments to "ignore the haters."

If our souls were made for blessing, it's no wonder that anything that feels like a curse can be such an anathema to our sense of self-worth. It makes sense.

Substitutes Don't Work

Our souls desire blessing like our bodies thirst for water. We are yearning for the blessing that will satisfy us. If we don't accept the blessing God is extending to us, we look for substitutes. We keep hoping those substitutes will work, but they keep not working.

Maybe you've noticed that while we nearly all think we're upstanding, better-than-average, good people, we still wonder if we're good enough at all. For example, talk to any mom. In one context, she'll tell you she's a good mom, so don't judge her. In another context, she'll confide that she suspects she's failing.

> Maybe you've noticed that while we nearly all think we're upstanding, better-than-average, good people, we still wonder if we're good enough at all.

I know many men like this too, of course. I wrote about the "imposter syndrome" in my last book, *Blessed Are the Misfits*, and how I suffer from it myself. Many of the most seemingly confident people in the world are afraid others will find out their little secret: They're not good enough. They don't really know what they're doing. They're afraid they'll be exposed.

We're complicated creatures, capable of great contradictions. We can militantly defend our rightness while simultaneously wondering, at the deepest level, if we have lasting value at all. Perhaps that's *why* we're so militant about this goodness thing. We keep trying to establish our moral credentials because we're trying to find security the hard way.

Into this exhausting, conflicting mess steps Jesus, who loves his lost sheep. And he tells us that doing things his way actually makes the burden lighter. He says he's coming for the sinners, not the "righteous" (Luke 5:32), and he's bringing us exactly what so many of us need: peace (see John 14:27).

Peace is what happens when our souls finally find what they're looking for. The real thing. No more counterfeit blessings. No more elaborate hiding schemes, weak ego-protecting excuses, or blaming others. There's no need, if we trust in the love of God instead of our goodness.

And you know what's also wonderful? I've noticed that when I'm not worried about my own virtuousness, I can finally focus on blessing other people, even those who curse me. It's actually more fun than it sounds.

We can approach each person with a fundamental question in mind: How can I add value to this person's life?

> We can approach each person with a fundamental question in mind: How can I add value to this person's life?

Here's an example: Our neighborhood has a little workout room, and consistently, no matter what time I use it, a particular guy comes in and starts playing his music. Then he starts huffing and puffing, presumably to get himself psyched before a big lift. And he takes his shirt off, showing off his medallion. He grunts and drops his weights. It's like he's taken the time to figure out, in great detail and with great precision, how to be Most Annoying Gym Guy, and he's executing the plan perfectly.

Man, he bugged me. I thought about having it out with him but then thought better of it. So I tried something else: I forced myself to pray for him while I was on the ellipti-cal machine. And when I saw him in the hallway the next time, I told him I admired how hard he worked out and mentioned I could use a little more of that intensity in my own exercise.

He was very kind. Now when I see him, he smiles and says, "Hey." He still plays his music and grunts, but that doesn't bother me anymore. My attitude has completely changed. I decided to bless him in the smallest way and not go on cursing him. Suddenly I'm *for* him.

A few years ago, a similar thing happened . . . at another fitness center. (Honestly, I'm not that into fitness. I'm not sure why this keeps happening.) The manager of the place hated me. It was palpable. I don't know why, but even other people picked up on it. It was comical.

When Christmas season rolled around, I forced myself to buy the manager a Starbucks gift card and write him a small note, thanking him for all his work. I told him I knew that being a manager can be a thankless job, but my wife and I so appreciated all his effort in making the gym a nice place to be. His work mattered to us.

His attitude changed immediately and permanently. When I'd walk in, he'd call out my name and wave from his desk. I went from dreading seeing him to asking God to bless him and his work. I actually suddenly cared. I hadn't before.

These are such trivial-sounding examples, I know. But blessing people—adding value to their lives—matters. And as I learn more about doing the things Jesus said, the more I realize that it's life-giving.

Blessings or curses. It's up to us. I've found that I'm freed up to be a blessing to people when I am no longer expending my energy defending myself.

Am I a good person? A horrible person? What's my moral ranking? How about this: Who cares? What I want—what we want—more than anything isn't actually to be *right*. It's to be blessed. It's to be secure, significant, and loved. There's no avoiding this. It's part of our internal logic, our source code.

I need to believe and remember that God has blessed me. And then I want to be a blessing to people.

God has added infinite value to our lives. He has a beautiful future in mind for us. He has publicly proclaimed our value to him, our worthiness of blessings. And he has blessed us, indeed.

NINE

Hide the Bud Light Towel: Adventures in Guilt

Battling Self-Righteousness by Getting Off the Guilt Trip

> When we played softball, I'd steal second base, feel guilty and go back.
>
> —Woody Allen

When I was a kid being raised in fundamentalist churches, religious guilt and shame were never more than an inch away. I remember preachers saying things like, "What if Jesus wanted to come to your house . . . this very day? How embarrassed would you be about what he'd find?"

Hmmm.

"Would there be magazines you'd be embarrassed were on the coffee table? Better pick those up. Wouldn't he be disgusted by your copy of *TV Guide*?" (By the way, that was an actual little magazine that told us what was on each of our three channels, and . . . no one's going to understand this.)

"Would he see the beach towel with the beer company logo? Hmmm? What then?"

Whatever you do, don't let Jesus see the Bud Light towel. *You guys, hide the Bud Light towel from Jesus.*

I shifted in my pew next to my mom, wondering if Jesus would be offended when he found the Lincoln Logs I merely shoved under my bed when I was supposed to be cleaning my room. I would be so busted. And worse, I wondered—especially after puberty—*What if I met Jesus, and he knew my actual dirty thoughts? I almost can't NOT have dirty thoughts, especially when I'm trying not to have dirty thoughts! I'm full of dirty thoughts, and Jesus is going to know it, and he'll walk out before he can even be offended by the Lincoln Logs.*

I hated this scenario.

There's this guy I met once with a really interesting job. He's a therapist to celebrities. Nashville musicians, mainly. Artists who are marketed to Christians as well as big-time country music headliners.

I asked him, "What is it they're really looking for? I mean, really, what do these people, who are always being applauded and admired, feel like they're missing?"

He didn't hesitate. "That's easy," he said. "They want me to know them. The real them. They want someone, anyone, to truly know them and love them anyway."

Makes sense. They perform, and even when they're applauded, they know it's not the real them being applauded. It's sort of them, but a much better version. They have lights and smoke and real-time pitch correction. We all look cooler with lights-n-smoke. (Product idea: Personal, Portable Lights-n-Smoke Set.)

And here's the problem for musicians marketed to Christians: You have to deal with the internal dissonance of your own sinfulness versus the impression you know you're giving people. You will hear from your conscience. You can either ignore it and do what so many high-profile (and low-profile!) professing believers do, which is rationalize, compartmentalize, and live a double life. Or you can be overrun with guilt, wondering deep down how God could possibly love you, the big-stage Christian hypocrite.

> We can really believe that God knows our thoughts, the very dirtiest, the most hateful, vile, unloving, dishonest, traitorous ones . . . and still loves us.

Thankfully—because, let's face it, we're all performers—there's a third option: We can really believe that God knows our thoughts, the very dirtiest, the most hateful, vile, unloving, dishonest, traitorous ones . . . and still loves us. Not "loves" as in *tolerates*, or "loves" as in *merely sees how pathetic we are and doesn't zap us*. I mean "loves" as in *loves*.

This stuff is all over the Bible too:

"Jesus knew their thoughts and . . ." (Matt. 12:25).
"Jesus, knowing their evil intent . . ." (Matt. 22:18).

"Jesus knew what they were thinking and . . ." (Luke 6:8).

"Jesus knew their thoughts and . . ." (Luke 11:17).

And . . . wanted to be with them.

And . . . gave himself up for them.

And . . . loved them.

He hung around a bunch of dirty-minded men, saw right through them, and then told them he was going to prepare a place for a big party . . . for them.

Once, Jesus invited himself over to the home of a notorious sinner, a "chief tax collector," whom apparently no one liked. It shocked the neighbors. They couldn't believe it. While we don't have many details, the Bible says the sinner "welcomed him gladly" and was profoundly impacted, excitedly declaring he would pay back everything he had cheated from people, and then some. Maybe Jesus went through the house, looking for offensive items, but I don't get that impression from the text. It seems like they both really enjoyed the visit (see Luke 19:1–10).

That's just one incident, of course, and the more I read about Jesus, the more I suspect that if he came to my house today, he'd know my thoughts and think, "Yep, that's a human. I love humans."

He'd see my kids' paintings and photos and my puppets, and we'd make some toast. And he'd see our magnet with a photo of John, Paul, George, and Ringo, and maybe he'd talk about how much he loves them too.

I'd be thinking, *What? He knows my selfishness and terrible thoughts and all my time-wasting, and . . . he'll still talk to me? About my puppets, no less?*

It's funny how grace turns everything upside down. If I'm trying to avoid God with my goodness or impress him with it, the fact that he knows what I'm thinking becomes a frightful one. But if I'm humble, if I already know I'm busted, that fact goes from frightful to *the best news ever*.

Why? Because he knows us, all about us, and he still loves us.

That's why the message of this book isn't about guilt for being woefully human. It's about living in the reality that we are loved by Someone who already knows the truth about us.

Virtue Signaling Is an International Sport

We professing Christians are known for being self-righteous. But it's also true that we aren't monopolizing the market. This sickness, this delusion, this desire to see ourselves as more virtuous than others, is something everyone suffers from. It's pan-cultural. It spans the world and all demographics.

How do I know this? Well, for starters: Facebook. I actually have this vision of a planning session for angels that was held back in 2003:

> Facilitator: We need a way to prove to humanity its own fallenness, its own unending, pathetic search for approval, its bottomless neediness, and its preening self-righteousness. If only there was some—
>
> Out of nowhere, Mark Zuckerberg: Hi, excuse me, I have an idea.

And of course, we have Twitter too. Here's a (slightly altered) example of an actual tweet I read:

> Pulled up at a 7-11 and found my neighbor's little boy from our neighborhood crying. His friends inside the store had money for a treat, but he didn't. So I bought him a Snickers. He was so happy! We sat and laughed while he ate. It's so good to be aware of needs and really help people. Empathy is what this world needs.

Okay, so this person wants us to know about her good deed. She bought a boy a treat! Now, the question is, how should we respond to this brazen treat-buying?

(A) No reaction; just move on.
(B) Think, *That's nice*, and click "Like" to encourage the writer.
(C) Rally a vigilante group for a full-on, frontal attack.

The correct answer is (C), because we're us.
Here's one response:

> Okay, I have to step in here. A Snickers bar contains eggs and milk, and I noticed in this person's profile that she is a "committed vegan." This is the type of person who is hurting the cause of animals she claims to care about. Please send a message that this sort of ignorant behavior will not be tolerated. She should be ashamed of herself.

Yes, to my knowledge, humans are alone among creatures who possess the ability to take a story about buying a treat for a kid and turn it into a bad deed. Even dolphins can't do this, and they can do everything.

We humans need to signal our virtue, hoping to be affirmed in our rightness, but you know what? It's never quite good enough. It's a never-ending game, and it's played by seemingly everybody. It reaches from left to right and everywhere in the middle. Feminist Flavia Dzodan identifies it in what she calls "call out culture."

> [Call out culture] works more or less like this: I say something ignorant. . . . Unbeknown to me, there are now ten posts in ten different blogs and social media platforms calling me a "BIGOT AND THE WORST PERSON EVER." . . . Each new post trying to outperform the previous one in outrage, in anger, in righteousness. . . . The intent behind it, more often than not, is *just to make the one initiating the call out feel good*, more righteous, more indignant, a "better person."[1]

> We humans need to signal our virtue, hoping to be affirmed in our rightness, but you know what? It's never quite good enough.

Ah, yes. This is where it ultimately goes: The more indignant we are about other people, the better we can feel about ourselves. Helen Andrews, a managing editor for the *Washington Examiner*, writes about this in an essay called "Shame Storm":

> The more online shame cycles you observe, the more obvious the pattern becomes: Everyone comes up with a principled-sounding pretext that serves as a barrier against admitting

to themselves that, in fact, all they have really done is join a mob.[2]

Our shared addiction to being "right" and "good" is one of those things that, once seen, we can't unsee. We'll notice self-righteousness everywhere, and all this noticing is a very annoying thing, because we'll also notice it in ourselves.

Annoying, yes, but also wonderful, especially if it leads us to stop finding fault with everyone else in our lives. *We need to see how dwelling on others' shortcomings or sins is simply feeding our addiction to our favorite myth.*

This is why our gossip is both so very human and so immensely destructive. In the Bible, Peter writes that believers are to "love each other deeply, because love covers over a multitude of sins" (1 Pet. 4:8). Gossip seems like the very opposite of sin-covering.

We're also told in Scripture that those of us who are believers in Jesus are to confess our sins to one another. It immediately humbles us and reminds us of our own need of forgiveness, and that tempers our criticism of others. I need that, because I've noticed this: If I don't confess my own sins, I will confess yours.

I find it very difficult to confess my own sins to anyone. But complaining about what other people do? That seems to flow so naturally.

Forgetful People

As much as we want to believe we are good people, and whatever we claim to believe about God, the way we act seems to suggest that we all suspect there's a yawning, terrible gap between us and true goodness. We want to traverse it ourselves. We'll use our religious acts, our social justice commitments, our endless justifications and rationalizations—whatever we sense it might take. We'll even try to convince ourselves that the terrible thing, that deep separation, really isn't there after all.

Yet the sense persists. We continue to be driven by this more than anything else.

Until we run into the love of God. The one who wants us to finally acknowledge who we are and who he is. He knows us better than we know ourselves and still finds us extremely worthwhile.

It's so hard for many of us to really believe it, to really let it soak in: Our value to God isn't determined by our goodness at all. He loves us because that's what he does. He loves.

Yes, I've heard that a thousand times, and maybe you have too. But it's only when I begin to believe it that I can not only admit I'm not a "good person" but do it joyfully, knowing my value isn't attached to my morality.

I often struggle to believe. I forget. I need to be reminded: "Brant, God actually loves you. He's for you. He's not a cosmic sheriff waiting to blast you with his six-shooter in the sky."

I need people around me to demonstrate his love. I've never been a good pray-er, but I need to keep communicating with him. I need to keep opening my Bible and reading stories about how he operates. I'm a forgetful person.

I know I'm not alone. Honestly, I think we believe God loves us, yes, but we still struggle with self-righteousness because we're forgetful people.

When I actually confess my sins, I'm reminded that God still loves me. I can breathe it in again. And I can stop being so judgmental of others and myself.

There's a semi-famous story of a man (Will Campbell, in his autobiography) whose friend wanted him to sum up Christianity. He didn't want another long, complex explanation. Could Will do it in less than ten words?

Will came up with this: "We're all bastards but God loves us anyway."[3]

His friend told him he could try again, since he had two words left. But I think Campbell did a pretty good job. "God loves us anyway" means *he's* the one spanning the terrible gap. We can't do it, try as we might, and almost everyone is trying.

We can deal with guilt in a thousand destructive, indirect ways. We can try to ignore it, sublimate it, or rationalize it away, or we can come clean and ask for forgiveness.

What's Guilt For?

I once asked a friend about guilt. He's old and has a beard, so maybe that contributes to the effect, but he's someone I genuinely consider wise. He's a very forgiving person who's easy to be around. I asked him, "When is guilt good? Is it ever good?"

He told me that yes, guilt can be good, but only for a very short time—enough to drive us right back to Jesus. "That's what the cross was for. It paid for that," he said. "Our guilt should remind us of the cross, and . . . that's the end of it. Be humble and take it there, and you don't have to carry it around anymore. Life gets healthier."

I see what he means now.

I'll speak for myself here. I think when I'm at my most self-righteous, it's not because I sense that I'm especially pure. I suspect it's because I'm struggling to handle my guilt by myself.

There's a concept called *moral licensing*, where we give ourselves moral credit in some area to compensate for a moral deficit in another, or let ourselves slack in one area because we think we're doing such a great job in another. Too often, growing up in church, I listened to very legalistic sermons from men who would later be caught for any number of indecencies. I now listen to moral tirades—whether they're about sex or recycling—with a good deal of "Hmmm. What's really going on, I wonder?"

"No one is good," Jesus says. And judging by the biblical stories, no one who thinks they're good is in good standing with God. So, is the gospel—the Good News about the kingdom of God—actually a guilt trip? I think it's the opposite.

You see, the world is *already* on a guilt trip, even if it's unacknowledged. Everyone is aboard the Guilt Train, and Jesus is the only way off.

TEN

Let's Freak People Out

Battling Self-Righteousness by Staying Together

> [Christians] are a band of natural enemies who love one another for Jesus' sake.
>
> —D. A. Carson

If you're like me, you realize you need a community of honest, loving people to help you with your self-righteousness problem. Unfortunately, this is hard work. If they're not put off immediately by my puppet collection, they will eventually find something else about me that's tough to take. This is the nature of things.

I can put our problem in riddle form: "What do the Beatles, my parents, and the '04 Lakers have in common?"

And the answer is, unsurprisingly, "They couldn't stay together."

They all broke up. They just couldn't take it anymore.

This is not abnormal. This is the natural state of things. Shaq and Kobe could've dominated for a decade, but they couldn't stand each other anymore. The Beatles told us that all we need is love, but then they couldn't take it anymore and they broke up screaming.

Things fall apart.

My parents? Like millions of Americans, they got divorced. That marriage is hard shouldn't be a surprise. (First clue: Anything that starts with you taking a vow in front of hundreds not to quit? That's going to be hard.)

In fact, staying together at *anything* is hard. Sure, bands (think about it: *band* means they're bound together) like the Eagles or the Police can get back together for a big money-making reunion tour, but the tension on stage is palpable.

We humans want to "imagine" a world where everyone can "give peace a chance," and yet the Beatles themselves turned into what Paul McCartney says was an "unhealthy rivalry."[1] McCartney's a poet, and "unhealthy rivalry" is a pithy way to put it. It's tragic that this dynamic is far more characteristic of humanity than the vision in "Imagine."

After all the poetry and profound imagery and leading of a peace movement, the band dissolved in acrimony. John Lennon concluded in an angry letter to McCartney that, in the final analysis, the Beatles were "just as big [jerks] as anyone else."[2]

Nailed it. You wrote great songs, but doggone it, you're just like the rest of us, guys. Something's deeply wrong with the self-righteous lot of us.

This is why utopian communities never work. No matter the good intentions, no matter the education level of the participants, no matter the organizational ability, they all share the same fate. It's just a matter of time. This is because they have something in common: humans.

There's an old song called "Breaking Up Is Hard to Do," and it's got a point. But you know what's harder? Staying together.

Disintegration isn't remarkable. Entropy isn't remarkable. Disunity isn't remarkable. Unity is.

This is why I want to ask my fellow professing Christians to do something downright shocking in today's online environment: *Be radically charitable to your Christian brothers and sisters.* Be downright deferential. Consider them better than you. Demonstrate humility and love in every interaction.

Do not insult their intelligence. Do not mock them. Do not presume them to be beneath your sophistication. Assume the best of their intentions. Do not belittle them. If you want to engage their ideas and disagree, do so.

> There's an old song called "Breaking Up Is Hard to Do," and it's got a point. But you know what's harder? Staying together.

Find something they've said you can agree with, and comment on it. Offer a quick, genuine prayer for them and their family before you comment. Consider a direct message rather than a public comment to engage a discussion. That alone will defuse much tension.

If they get testy with you or put you down, consider how you can encourage them. (If that sounds too far-out, imagine the reaction people had to Jesus when he said to bless those who curse us.)

Remember that few online arguments actually solve anything. Don't expect their next comment to be, "You're right!

I've seen the light!" As we've seen, that's not how people work.

Consider what Paul wrote to believers in Rome who had serious disagreements: "Let us therefore make every effort to do what leads to peace" (Rom. 14:19). He told the Corinthians that even if we're saying wonderful things, even if we're doing wonderful things, but we're not doing them out of love, we're just annoying noise (see 1 Cor. 13:1–4).

Remember your own status as someone who has failed and needed rescuing. Offer forgiveness to others because of what God has done for you, whether they deserve it or not.

Does this sound hard to do? Of course, because it is hard to do. Hard doesn't mean complex, though. It's simple to understand. It's hard to humble ourselves and serve others. But this is exactly what following Jesus looks like and has always looked like.

This needn't stop reasoned debate. But let kindness mark every exchange. Start with kindness and end with kindness.

Here's why:

1. **The world is watching us, and they would be freaked out.** If we actually modeled unity, it would be a bolt of stunning grace from out of the blue. No one expects this. No one else is doing it. People would wonder how it is that we could possibly get along. *What's making them stick together? They clearly disagree with each other, yet they are so loving even when they are debating? What gives?*

    Everything else falls apart. *So why don't they?*

2. **Jesus said unity is what will prove to the world that we belong to him** (see John 17:22–23). This is the

very hallmark of who we are. Not our enlightened bumper stickers, not our issue-of-the-day tweets, not our big church stage shows. (In fact, a friend of mine had the temerity to suggest that perhaps we like big stage shows, political posturing, and debating other issues so much precisely *because* we are failing so bitterly at Jesus' priority of unity. She might be onto something.)

You see, if we don't fall apart, we're very strange indeed. Something supernatural surely must be at work. It's like we're defying gravity. How is it possible?

Unity based on absolute agreement is not supernatural. But if we genuinely disagree, even vehemently disagree, yet model love and deference in all of our public and private communications, well, that's another thing entirely. What could possibly explain that?

Who are these weirdos who love like that?

I propose we all model this immediately. Again, this isn't rendering issues unimportant. This isn't short-circuiting debate. It's simply shaping how we do it.

Look, I'm a logic machine. I think quickly. (A doctor friend of mine laughingly said he wants to avoid arguments with me for fear of again being "logically pummeled.") But if I have not love—love that endures—I'm a bunch of noise.

As brutal as social media is, that's where people are. Instead of using it to tear each other to shreds for the benefit of our political allies, maybe we could use it as a place to demonstrate what a city on a hill looks like. Disagree with a brother or sister? It will happen. But these people are our family above all.

After all, if someone else calls Jesus "Lord" in this increasingly post-Christian culture, it means something. Fifty years ago, it may not have meant so much to say such a thing. But things have changed, and now acknowledging that there is a King who transcends us, and it's Jesus of Nazareth—that's a big deal. If we agree on that, we may not vote together, but we can sing together and pray together and talk together. We have a bond that's deeper than public policy, deeper than our misunderstandings, deeper than our wounds.

Things fall apart. But we don't have to.

As Paul said, "He is before all things, and in him all things hold together" (Col. 1:17).

Back to Eden

If we were naturally good and Jesus was wrong about the "evil" business, staying together wouldn't be so hard.

Even if we won't acknowledge sin, even if we won't give it a name, we hope to fix it. We hope we can buy the right book, go to the right conference, study the right religious system, or watch the right TED Talks. The Dalai Lama said the fix-all is meditation. "If every 8 year old in the world is taught meditation, we will eliminate violence from the world in one generation," he said, in a statement that ignores Buddhists' key roles in bloody conflicts and hatred.[3]

I certainly understand the hope. We all yearn for what he's yearning for. Even people who don't believe in the stories of Genesis seem to have internal compasses pointing them back to Eden. We're all trying to get back.

Some people hope to find what they're looking for at Burning Man. If you're not familiar with it, it's an arts festival that draws more than sixty thousand each year to the desert in Nevada. Burning Man's own website talks about the inevitable letdown of the people who think they're going to find Eden, a place where people are suddenly different, and a society that is finally fair and loving:

> The people who I've seen have the hardest times reconciling themselves to what Burning Man really is are the utopians— the people who at some level believe that Burning Man really is a place that changes everything. . . .
>
> Of course it isn't like that. . . .
>
> There is no enlightenment spell, and the absolutely saddest thing I have ever seen on the playa are people who are desperately lonely who come to Burning Man thinking "once I get there, I'll have lots of friends." . . .
>
> The people who do last are the ones who (to borrow a metaphor) see within the miraculous things that happen here a calling to pick up their own cross.[4]

It's striking that the Burning Man writer turns to Jesus' phrasing when describing how it is that we might actually flourish. He's alluding to Luke 9, where Jesus says, "Whoever wants to be my disciple must deny themselves and take up their cross daily and follow me" (v. 23).

My smart friend Barry tells me that the Greek word for *deny* is only used in a couple contexts in the New Testament. In this context, Jesus tells us to deny ourselves, and in the other context, Jesus gives Peter the chilling news that "Before the rooster crows, you will deny Me three times" (Luke 22:61 NKJV).

If Smart Barry is right, Jesus isn't talking about a subtle thing. He's talking about completely disavowing ourselves.

It's consistent with his message that if we want to find real life, we must first lose our own. "Whoever does not take up their cross and follow me is not worthy of me. Whoever finds their life will lose it, and whoever loses their life for my sake will find it" (Matt. 10:38–39).

If we're all basically good, why tell us to deny ourselves? Why casually refer to us as "evil"? You don't do that if you're convinced of the goodness of human nature. In fact, Jesus should demand the opposite—that we learn to affirm ourselves daily. Instead, he is telling us disavow ourselves, and we'll find real life.

Yes, it's tough to take, but wise people still want to hear it. When the truth really matters, we should want it. Like from doctors. If they told me, "Brant, if you eat another piece of toast, you will die immediately," I would give toast up forever, because images of my wife and kids would flash before me. Everyone who knows me knows I love toast dearly, but I love my family more. The point is, I want the truth. Denial kills.

This is the way to unity. For Jesus' sake, let's consider others better than ourselves. We're not looking to be offended. We're covering a multitude of others' sins. Yes, we tend to break apart, but he promises us we don't have to, and that our unity (if we choose it) will be evidence to the world that he is, in fact, King of Kings.

No one else can stick together very well, can they? If we make it work, it must be supernatural. And boy, do we need this unity thing to work. Not only did Jesus say our unity would prove we are sent by him, but as we've seen, we're just too broken to see things clearly without others. As Daniel Kahneman stresses, other people can see our errors when we can't. We simply can't trust our self-affirming, self-enhancing, self-righteous selves.

No wonder the book of Proverbs mentions this: "Where there is no guidance the people fall, but in abundance of counselors there is victory" (11:14 NASB).

Proverbs also adds this about humility and being willing to listen: "Through insolence comes nothing but strife, but wisdom is with those who receive counsel" (13:10 NASB).

Then there's this, just to drive the point home: "Listen to counsel and accept discipline, that you may be wise the rest of your days" (19:20 NASB).

And, "in abundance of counselors there is victory" (24:6 NASB). There's that too.

In case we missed the point, we get this in Proverbs 27: "Oil and perfume make the heart glad, so a man's counsel is sweet to his friend" (v. 9 NASB).

If we're not sick of this yet, Proverbs 15, thousands of years ago, said what cognitive scientists are telling us now: Don't delude yourself. Listen to the wise.

> He whose ear listens to the life-giving reproof
> Will dwell among the wise.
> He who neglects discipline despises himself,
> But he who listens to reproof acquires
>   understanding.
> The fear of the LORD is the instruction for wisdom,
> And before honor comes humility. (vv. 31–33 NASB)

Self-righteousness impedes our ability to listen. It thwarts our efforts to be in lasting relationships.

But humility is the very opposite of this. It relies on others.

It allows us to be corrected, to be set straight. It opens us to wisdom.

I've learned the hard way that wisdom brings peace while foolishness brings pain. The Proverbs writer emphasizes another benefit: This wisdom, born of humility and however tough to take at first, leads to a great night's sleep!

> My son, do not let wisdom and understanding out
>   of your sight,
>   preserve sound judgment and discretion;
> they will be life for you,
>   an ornament to grace your neck.
> Then you will go on your way in safety,
>   and your foot will not stumble.
> When you lie down, you will not be afraid;
>   when you lie down, your sleep will be sweet. (Prov.
>   3:21–24)

ELEVEN

The Worst Wonderful Word

Battling Self-Righteousness with Refreshing Repentance

> The good life starts with an apology.
>
> —Jen Oshman

There are a lot of words that people don't like. I just looked at a Most Hated Words list, and the usual suspects are at the very top: *moist*, *ululate*, and—obviously—*giblets*.[1]

I'm going to guess *repent* is up there pretty high too. It's an extremely religious-sounding word, it sure isn't affirming, and—like *giblets*—we all expect *repent* will be eventually yelled at us by an apocalyptic sandwich board guy.

Here's another annoying thing about repentance: For all the talk about it, not many people actually do it. Even in the Bible, there's more talking about repentance than actual repenting.

Repent means to rethink and turn around. In the case of this book's topic, there's a strong internal resistance to that when it means turning away from ourselves and our perceptions of our own goodness.

We don't do it naturally. What comes naturally is everything *but* repentance. What comes naturally to us are all the blame-avoidance techniques and cognitive shortcuts we've been discussing, and so many more.

Repentance is, above all, just plain weird. It freaks people out when it's real.

The other day, I watched a point guard on a Big Ten basketball team correct the refs. He told them that he, not the other team, had last touched the ball before it went out of bounds. The refs seemed perplexed, but they reversed their call and gave it to the other team.

No one knew what to do with this. Fans of both teams were slack-jawed. Who *does* that? That's odd.

Repentance is kind of like that. It's profound, and also just strange. It's highly unnatural, unorthodox, and largely untried. It's also traffic-stopping. It causes a disturbance in the Force.

And wow, is it beautiful.

The Rarity of Repentance

One hint that real repentance doesn't happen often: Jesus stresses more than once that there's a big party in heaven if just one sinner repents. "There is rejoicing in the presence of the angels of God over one sinner who repents," he says (Luke 15:10). Just one. He's telling stories, and he says, effectively, "When just one of you people finally, actually, for-real, truly humbles yourself, we party like it's 1999 AD."

Repentance is that rare.

The *New York Times* recently ran a story about a young man who repented. Derek Black was a white nationalist who'd learned much from his father, one of the leaders of the movement in the US. Derek was intelligent, committed to the cause, and, in his mind, quite logical. But when he left for college, he was invited to dinner with a Jewish student. The other guests were a diverse lot. They put up with Derek despite his ideas. There were long conversations, deep arguments, and, above all, extended and patient kindness.[2]

Ultimately, Derek broke with his past. He couldn't continue to hate people who extended hospitality and friendship to him. It was excruciating, and it took time, but he did it. Good for him.

By the way, Derek's story wasn't just in the *New York Times*. It was also on NPR. It was in the *New York Post* too. And on *Oprah*. Plus the *Daily Beast*, *Christianity Today*, *Huffington Post*, *The Today Show*. . . . It's been everywhere.

If repentance, or repudiating ourselves, were a normal thing, well, it probably wouldn't be headline news. "Guy We Hadn't Previously Heard of Actually Rethinks, Goes the Other Way" wouldn't crawl across the bottom of a screen.

It's so difficult (putting it mildly) to put off family traditions, our own one-sided readings, our pet tribal biases, and our faith in our own intellects, but Derek managed to do it. It's a testament to the power of relationship.

In fact, relationship may be the only thing that leads us to turn around. It's just so very hard to repent. There's really no way to do it, unless we can replace the things we love with something, or someone, we love even more.

Repentance requires a lot of things, including this: We simply can't be in denial anymore. Denial, by the way, has an almost absurdly strong hold on us. As we've seen, when we're hit with reality we just can't process, we quickly unlearn that reality. One of the most common responses to a terminal diagnosis is simply denying it or forgetting about it within a few days.[3]

Repentance means no more convenient storywriting in our heads to avoid the truth about us. No more ignoring what we did. We have to face it and look at it and not turn away. We have to own it.

And wow, is that hard when you have to fight your own brain to do it. Seriously. MRI scans have shown that when we're hit with dissonant information—things we'd rather not know, things that disagree with our internal stories—the reasoning part of our brain starts to shut down and the emotional part starts lighting up.

Once again, we see how we don't process information well when it's counter to what we want to believe. As Kathleen Schulz observes, even when people who have falsely accused others (many of whom are sent to prison for decades) are faced with overwhelming evidence of how wrong they were, very few of them have "what have I done?" moments.[4]

Fauxpologies

Recently, I was in England with my son, and we waited impatiently for the bus to Oxford. When it finally arrived, I handed my credit card to the bus driver, and he told me it was cash only. We had to sheepishly get off the bus.

Maybe you've had a moment or three like that. It's a little disorienting, those few seconds after you're told that what you thought would get you somewhere isn't actually going to get you anywhere. I've spent my adult life building a decent credit rating, and I know my card is worth the $20 or so for a bus ticket. But in that moment, what I thought I had to offer was worthless. What do you mean my good credit doesn't even matter? I was frustrated and defensive and muttered, "You gotta be kidding me," like it was someone else's fault.

It's a mildly embarrassing and forgettable little story, but it's telling that my instinct, even in the smallest matters, is to defend myself, deflect, and immediately find someone else to blame.

You've likely noticed the proliferation of public apologies, or "fauxpologies," that hint at this too. There's the classic "mistakes were made" apology, which puts things in a passive voice, deflecting from the real problem.

Or, with a slight twist, you can seemingly own what you did but still refer to it as a "mistake," even if it's something you spent years plotting. ("Whoops, I made a mistake and blundered into a seamless *Ocean's 11*–style casino heist.") It wasn't a mistake; it was an act of the will, and you made it happen.

"I shouldn't have had an affair. To err is human, and I erred." No, you didn't err. A second baseman makes an error. A man who cheats on his wife did not make an error. You did exactly what you set out to do.

Then there's the "ifpology," when you say something like, "If anyone was hurt by that thing I did, I sincerely apologize." It allows you to subtly pass the blame forward, or at least share it, and evade total responsibility.

I'm good at these, by the way—these apologies that shift the blame. Let's say I say something stupid on the air, and someone is hurt and calls me on it in an angry email. I can easily "apologize" like this:

Please accept my sincere, deepest apologies for what you thought you heard me say the other day on the air, and the distress it no doubt caused your family when they heard you misquote it to them. It is my sincere commitment in the future to do a better job of making sure people listen more closely to my program, and a better job of attracting only listeners with reasonable comprehension skills.

Apologies are plentiful, but real repentance is rare and precious. That's because repentance is total. It's not a graduated thing. Jesus presents it to us as a binary: Either we go this way or that. Either we go our own way, on a path that seems right but leads to death, or the narrow way that leads to life.

Please think about the following verse. It's welcome news for some, yes, but it's simply a deal breaker for most: "The sacrifice you desire is a broken spirit. You will not reject a broken and repentant heart, O God" (Ps. 51:17 NLT).

> Repentance is total. It's not a graduated thing. Jesus presents it to us as a binary: Either we go this way or that.

Wait, so God wants a *broken* spirit? He wants to *break* my spirit?

Look, I'm an American man. I'm supposed to be a strong, free spirit. I want to be an unbroken, untamed, wild stallion riding my Harley willy-nilly over the western grasslands or wherever, doing whatever the heck I want.

But he wants me broken? Right now. Not later. It's hard to take. *Break my spirit?*

This is what it means to repent, and nothing less: *God, I give up. I'm yours. I'm giving up the show, I'm giving up the ego stories and protection mechanisms. I'm only fit to serve in your kingdom, if you'll let me.*

Repentance means finally coming to grips with this and, like a once untamed horse, giving in to the Master. In this case, the Master is very, very good. He doesn't want us to miss out on something beautiful.

Magical Kingdoms

We see that the kingdom of heaven really is all about God's authority in every area. Our relationships, our sex lives, our money, everything, now subject to his authority instead of ours. In retrospect, this shouldn't be shocking given that it is called a *kingdom*, and you can't have a kingdom without a king. Jesus never wavers on this. It's a big deal.

In fact, it's the biggest deal. The kingdom is Jesus' favorite topic. He talks more about the kingdom than anything else. He tells stories about it so we can understand it, shows what it looks like in real life by healing the sick, and keeps it in front of his ministry at all times.

All cultures understand the idea of a king and a kingdom. We even have a Magic Kingdom near where I live, and it's truly magical. Anything can happen. A mouse can talk! A boy can fly! An order of chicken fingers can be $25! The possibilities are limitless. It's magical. (By the way, a commenter on Reddit noted that Disney World is actually a human trap built by a mouse. I'm still mulling this over. Please think about it later.)

The point is, the kingdom of God is where *he* is in charge and things work the way he wants them to. From Jesus' descriptions, it's a beautiful place. He healed people to let us see an advance trailer for what the kingdom looks like.

And this kingdom is only open to the broken who acknowledge the King, not religious poseurs or enlightened do-gooders. Prostitutes are often closer to the kingdom than learned, upstanding citizens. I know this because Jesus said so.

Learned, upstanding citizens get to carry on the charade a little longer—the "I'm a good person" act—and do it in a convincing way, at least to themselves. But obvious moral failures? They've got an advantage. They're closer to embracing the kind of humility that allows for a contrite, broken spirit.

Oh, sure, we can pretend we're sinners. But if we're still claiming we're good people, we don't really believe that. Brennan Manning wrote, "At Sunday worship, as in every dimension of our existence, many of us pretend to believe we are sinners. Consequently, all we can do is pretend to believe we have been forgiven. As a result, our whole spiritual life is pseudo-repentance and pseudo-bliss."[5]

Yes, God wants our spirits broken, because if they're not broken, we will still be our own ultimate authority. That means we will not want to enter the kingdom of God. We will opt for the kingdom of me.

There's an unforgettable *Twilight Zone* episode that's about this, strangely enough. A guy goes to the afterlife and loves it. He's where he gets everything he wants. He gets the best cigars, all the women fawn over him, and he wins every pool or poker game he plays. He's in heaven, surely. He's always winning, winning, winning. It's always about him. It's everything he's ever wanted.

Until it's not. The days begin to drag, one after another. He becomes aware of the pointlessness of his existence. He's stuck inside what he thought would be his own fantasy, and it's grinding misery. The twist at the end? He's not where he originally thought he was at all. You wanted the kingdom of you, sir. There's another name for that, and it's not heaven.

The Joy of Forgiveness

This is going to sound silly and unimportant, but that's kind of the point.

When I was ten, I checked out a book from our little town library about a baseball player, Carl Yastrzemski. For some reason, I didn't get on my bike and return it after I'd read it. I just left it under my bed.

The thing was, even as I ignored it, it was still there, and I knew it. I felt increasingly nauseous about it. But I did nothing. I couldn't bear even thinking about the math (how much would my fine be by now?), and I certainly didn't want to tell anyone about it. So the book remained there.

Increasingly, I was racked with guilt. After months, I couldn't take it anymore. I'd been given $5 for my birthday, and I took the cash and the book and got on my bike.

When I went to the front desk of the library, I was almost crying. The lady told me the fine was more than $5 . . . and that I didn't need to worry about it. "It's okay. Just remember to bring back your books next time."

I was in awe. I distinctly remember the trip home on my bike. The autumn air, the handlebars, everything.

Not earth-shattering, is it? Breaking story: "Ten-Year-Old Finally Brings In Book, Catches Break at Town Library." No, it's not an amazing story, but here's the point: I remember it vividly. I was elated. I think I flew home on that bike, ET-style.

Repentance is rare and revolutionary and arduous and counter to our every instinct. It means reconsidering everything and reversing all the psychological machinery behind the easiest of all convictions: "It's someone else's fault."

But if we don't repent, we never get to feel the pure joy of forgiveness.

TWELVE

A Chainsaw at CVS

Battling Self-Righteousness with Desperation

> Ask people what they must do to get to heaven and most reply,
> "Be good." Jesus' stories contradict that answer. All we must
> do is cry, "Help!"
>
> —Philip Yancey

So here's a quick "What would you do?" scenario.

You're at a CVS pharmacy. You're in a very long, very slow line. You're there to pick up your sick child's prescription. It's taking forever. It's frustrating. You're shifting your weight impatiently from side to side. This is getting ridiculous. Your kid needs this medicine.

That's when you hear a noise you didn't expect, a noise you hear at CVS only on truly special occasions.

A running chainsaw.

Everyone looks up. There's urgent yelling, and powder and construction material fall from the ceiling. Then some guys quickly rappel down from the ceiling and cut in front of the line. There's a hubbub, dust is everywhere, and you can't tell what's going on, but apparently, some people really, really needed a prescription for a friend. You also notice that CVS is—somehow—cool with it. The pharmacists happily fill the line cutters' prescription requests.

Everyone else is aggravated. *Wait, they honor the line cutters? They don't even say anything about the roof damage? What?*

What would I do? Well, my usual plan is (1) whining, followed by (2) more whining—first in my head, then with the people around me, and then to a CVS employee. I was in line. These people are destroying my local pharmacy. I should be served before them. This is clearly unfair.

There's a story very roughly similar to this in the Gospels. It's actually even weirder. A huge crowd surrounds Jesus in a private home, and the place is overrun with people who want Jesus to talk with them, debate with them, or heal their loved ones. Some men actually (surprise!) cut through the roof to lower a crippled man to Jesus.

Some scholars believe it was Peter's house. I'm guessing Peter was hoping Jesus would look up and at least say something like, "Uh . . . excuse me, guys? You can wait in line with everyone else. There were people here before you. They have needs too. Destroying my friend's house is very *not* cool. Fix it. Sheesh."

But he doesn't. He honors the line-cutting house manglers by doing exactly what they wanted. He heals their friend. And just in case we're confused as to why, it's recorded in

Luke 5: He did it because of the audacious faith of the man's friends who cut the hole in the roof (v. 20).

We all have our rules, our ideas of goodness, and our concept of what crowd decorum should look like. There were other people there to be healed, no doubt some waiting patiently with their own children for healing too. Jesus loved them all, of course. But he sent a clear message: *Desperation wins.*

It always does.

It's a theme that rings through everything Jesus said and did. Those who are at the very end of themselves, desperate enough to humbly throw themselves vulnerably at the feet of God, with no excuses, will find exactly what they're yearning for.

As we've noted, when we think we're "good," we don't hunger and thirst for righteousness. We're not desperate. But Jesus said those who do hunger and thirst for it will be filled (see Matt. 5:6).

"Good people" are couth. They are dignified. They look put together to others. They enhance their reputations.

Desperation is uncouth. It's undignified. It looks pathetic and weak to others. It's not reputation enhancing. It's naked, exposed, and brutally honest.

I learned this repeatedly as a teenager, as many of us did. Once, returning from a friend's house in the country late at night (I grew up in sparsely populated rural Illinois), I ran out of gas in the middle of nowhere. This was before mobile phones were common. I wound up running and walking in the dark for miles, approaching darkened farmhouses and hoping no one would shoot me when I knocked for help. I was exhausted and lost.

I finally came to a little town where there was a light on in a home. An older gentleman cracked open the door. He was very suspicious. I told him, "Sir, at this point, I will take whatever I can get, even if I have to run with it in my mouth and spit it in the gas tank."

This was thirty years ago. That man is still alive. I know because he introduced himself to me after I spoke at a church recently back home. We laughed, and he told me he remembered it well, how he drove the teenage me all over the countryside that night to help me find my car. He said he helped me because I made the joke about spitting the gas. "You scared me, but I helped because I could tell you were desperate."

It's obvious to me now. It always should have been, but I missed it. This is exactly what God is looking for from you and me.

It's not just the roof-cutting guys who are rewarded for their level of last-resort determination. We've already talked about the sinner with a horrible reputation who pushed her way, uninvited, into the home of a seemingly upright religious leader. She did it just to throw herself at Jesus' feet. She was violating practically every norm of society, all in one fell swoop. She crashed the dinner party of the elites and risked mockery to do it.

She was humiliated by her sin. She fell to the floor, crying, washing Jesus' feet with her tears. Who does this? Desperate people, and no one else. She was vulnerable. She was at his mercy.

The host of the party thought Jesus must not be a prophet, because if he was, he'd know what an unclean mess this woman was. But Jesus did know. He defended her, and he lifted her desperation up as an example to the unrepentant "good" people (see Luke 7:36–50).

Another woman pushed through a crowd just to get to Jesus. She'd already bled for years, and she'd long been an unclean outcast from her community. She was already humiliated, so what did she have to lose? Would she just endure more isolation and mockery? Again: desperation. She'd been suffering for twelve years.

She managed to touch Jesus' clothes. When he asked who had touched him, she fell before him, trembling, in front of the crowd.

He gave her great news: She was healed, and her faith had done it. All that effort, all the indignity in that frantic attempt to get to him, was no reason to feel stupid.

She did exactly what she should have done, and what any of us should do. She did anything to get to Jesus.

"Go in peace," he told her (Luke 8:48).

Peace! Finally.

Desperation, when it goes to Jesus, leads to peace. If our supposed goodness keeps us from desperation, we'll never get there.

Another story: There's a guy named Zacchaeus who's well-known for being a rule-breaking jerk. Exactly zero (0) people like him. He's a cheat and a thief. A big crowd is assembled to see Jesus, but Zacchaeus is the one desperate enough to climb a tree to get a look at him. Don't think this was normal for adult men to do simply because it was two thousand years ago in a different culture. It wasn't. It's not a dignified look.

Jesus, the celebrity, scandalizes the crowd by making an announcement of where he's going for lunch: the home of the jerk in the tree.

The crowd mutters. "Doesn't he know who this guy is? Zacchaeus is stealing from us."

Yes, Jesus knows. The desperate, lonely cheater repents. Jesus seems ecstatic, and he announces again that this is why he's here: to save the lost (Luke 19:1–10).

Desperation wins again.

Remember the two men on crosses next to Jesus? One remains prideful and even manages to blame Jesus for his suffering. The other realizes he has absolutely nothing to offer, that his suffering is completely his own fault, and that Jesus is Lord. Jesus turns to the desperate one, the one emptied of pride, and says, "Today you will be with me in paradise" (Luke 23:43).

If we ever get achingly desperate enough to come to our senses, to come to the very end of ourselves, well . . . Jesus doesn't leave us hanging.

That's what repentance looks like, doing what the thief on the cross did: finally giving up the "I'm a good person" business and admitting the truth about us.

Desperately Seeking Desperation

So here's the equation: Bankrupt desperation leading to total submission to Jesus, and at the other end is . . . peace. This is how we get access to the kingdom of God. We can't experience that if we're still trying to be the king ourselves.

God shows us that people who give up the "I'm still the boss" business and submit to the rightful King will find the rest they've been yearning for. Jesus wants us to be childlike, and that comes with a lot of benefits, like realizing we can't control other people, for starters. What's more, we don't have to size up the goodness or badness of others or decide where they stand with God. We can just focus on today, trusting that there's a loving Father with a master plan. These are just some of the benefits of deciding to submit.

In the story of the prodigal son, we notice that Jesus isn't telling us the wayward son had to set up an appointment with his father. The story's audience would have expected the son to encounter the staff first, then have to go through his dad's butler or chief of staff just to get a message through. But there is no need, because the father sees him coming on the horizon. Dad was watching the whole time, just waiting.

> When I read the stories of Jesus, I can't help but see it: God is desperately waiting for us to be desperate.

We're always concerned about how we look. We want to hold on to our dignity. But there's not a lot of dignity in this story. Returning home a broken man? That's not dignifying. But neither is a patriarch running toward his son and embracing him before he can even apologize.

When I read the stories of Jesus, I can't help but see it: *God is desperately waiting for us to be desperate.*

I'm lucky to get to travel the world and visit CURE hospitals. CURE is the largest provider of pediatric surgeries in the developing world, and the hospitals are all about Jesus.

For a natural skeptic—someone who has seen the ugliness of commercialized "Christianity" up close and struggles with faith in general—these are restorative places for me. I feel like I get to see Jesus in action.

The hallways and waiting rooms and wards are full of abject desperation. Almost every mom who walks into a

CURE hospital is at her breaking point. If a woman gives birth to a child with a disability, she's often told the child is cursed—because of something *she* did. Very often, she is abandoned by the child's father. This is the norm in every country that CURE serves. People often run away screaming from the child, afraid that they will absorb the curse simply by being close.

The mother is often told to abandon or drown the child. She's kicked out of her community. She can afford nothing.

She hears something that could just be a rumor, about people who can heal her child. She gathers up her things, manages the money for a one-way bus ticket to the CURE hospital, and walks through the doors with nothing but her broken child.

Utterly, completely lonely. Desperate.

But because Jesus is here, remarkable things happen immediately.

No one runs away from her. Instead, for the first time in her child's life, she hears, "What a beautiful baby! Can I hold her?" from CURE nurses, doctors, receptionists, and housekeepers. Or "What a handsome boy! What is your name?"

But that's not even the best part. She's ushered into another room full of light and color. In that room she sees one of the most shockingly beautiful things she could possibly see: other moms, with other kids . . . who look like her child! The same problems, the same brokenness, the same stories.

The mom gets to hear stories of healing. She's told that she's not cursed at all. In fact, God draws close to the brokenhearted, and he has heard her cries. The pastoral staff tells her about a God who introduces himself this way: "I am the God who heals you."

There is music. Long conversations. The joy of seeing children—once isolated—giggling together.

Inside the children's ward, even before the child is wheeled into an operating room, heartbreak is turned to laughter.

"It's an instant sorority," my friend Ben, a pediatric surgeon, told me. "There's nothing else like it. Instant sisterhood."

Community is a wonderful thing. But there's nothing as deeply joyful, nothing as healing, as a community of the truly desperate.

"I Am My Own"

Honestly, it's astonishing how *not* desperate we Christians can be, how satisfied we can be with ourselves, in the face of all available evidence. Jesus claimed that the narrow way, the humble way, is a way few will choose, so perhaps it shouldn't be shocking. Yet it's at least alarming to see how we can take our cartoonish, grotesque pride to the grave with us. Maybe it's no surprise that the most popular song played at today's funerals is now "My Way."[1]

In 1996, Timothy McVeigh killed 168 people—including 19 children—in the Oklahoma City bombing. Before his execution, he made sure to be clear that he was still the boss. His last words recited the poem "Invictus," containing lines extolling his "unconquerable soul" and bragging that he remained "unbowed."

No, there would be no repentance. No desperation. McVeigh did it his way. The poem ends, and McVeigh's life ended, with, "I am the master of my fate. I am the captain of my soul."[2]

I say our pride is cartoonish because it really does become farcical. Earlier, I mentioned the trial of Adolf Eichmann, architect of the Nazis' "Final Solution" of annihilating the Jews. Eichmann tried to rationalize his role—he claimed he didn't personally kill anyone with his own hands. He did acknowledge that he had aided in mass murder.

Did he have any regrets? Was he sorry? Oh, no. Ironically, for a man who defended himself by claiming he was only following orders, he wanted to make sure we knew he was still in charge. "Repentance is for little children," he said.[3]

Our to-the-bitter-end need to elevate ourselves is tragicomical. We are infinitesimal, short-lived specks on an unimportant planet in an unremarkable solar system in one of billions of galaxies. For one of those specks to declare, "I am the captain!" before disappearing again into nothingness is really rather naive and not terribly impressive.

The brilliant writer George MacDonald once wrote, "The one principle of Hell is—'I am my own.'"[4]

Conversely, a principle of the kingdom is, "I am not my own." I am not the master of my fate. I am not the captain of my soul.

Oddly, perhaps, Eichmann is right: Repentance really is for little children. It's for anyone, really, who knows they're vulnerable. It's for people who know they can no longer defend themselves.

Repentance means no more attempts at self-justifying. No more rationalizing. No more excuses. No more artisan-crafted pseudo-apologies. No subtle blame shifting. No redefining the problem. No public, tearful apologies followed by attempts to save face.

Only humble people can pull this off.

Proud people are many things, but they are never desperate.

THIRTEEN

Seven Billion Italian Stallions

Battling Self-Righteousness and the Urge to Justify

> The human ego prefers anything, just about anything, to falling or changing or dying. The ego is that part of you that loves the status quo, even when it is not working. It attaches to past and present, and fears the future.
>
> —Richard Rohr

Let's talk about evil people.

I learned about evil people the usual way, the way most people do. By that, I mean I learned by reading Russian dissident Aleksandr Solzhenitsyn, sure, but mostly by watching the show *CHiPs*.

Now, Solzhenitsyn, through both his fiction and his writing about the Soviet gulag, helped me understand that evil is something we all have to do battle with. But *CHiPs*, through both its awesome motorcycles and its cool cops, offered a stark counterpoint: There really are just plain evil people, and they are pretty obvious to spot. Their mustaches are different. They drive vans. They rub their hands together when they're making plans. These are all giveaways. Plus they cackle with glee. That's when you know. Too much glee? Huge tip-off.

At this point in my life, I'm leaning toward Solzhenitsyn's impression of humanity. "If only it were all so simple!" he wrote. "If only there were evil people somewhere insidiously committing evil deeds, and it were necessary only to separate them from the rest of us and destroy them. But the line dividing good and evil cuts through the heart of every human being."[1]

We cartoonize evil in our pop culture to make it distinct from us. We want to believe bad people are obviously bad, and since I'm not obviously bad, I must be pretty good.

The other day I saw some ugly news on the Facebook page of a religious radio station. One of the on-air personalities had been arrested for abusing children. The comment thread was understandably full of shock and alarm. One comment: "Sure, we all sin, but there's a difference between sin and pure evil."

Right. I may sin, but I'm not one of the bad guys. Sounds reasonable enough.

Problem: The Jesus in Scripture doesn't ever tolerate that approach. He hates it. I can't find a single instance in the Bible of Jesus approving of someone thinking they're morally superior to anyone else. Not one. Whenever anyone tries it, he turns the tables on them. When the upstanding people pick up stones to throw at an adulteress, he defends her and challenges their own supposed goodness. He doesn't allow them to use comparisons to kid themselves about who they are.

Notice, too, how when real-life people don't fit the obviously evil profile in our heads and they do something horrific, we tend to say, "Wow, they must've just snapped," as though a seemingly inexplicable crime must be the result of a random synaptic breakdown.

"We don't just snap," a longtime professor of psychiatry told me. "We like to tell ourselves other people 'snap' to avoid the reality that they made decisions, and incremental decisions add up over time."

He told me this as I was interviewing him after a local news story about a mom who had stabbed and killed her son. Murders happened fairly often in our city, but this story was causing massive discussion and worry. Why? This particular mom had a doctorate. She was well-to-do, informed, and part of all the "right" causes locally. High-status associates jumped to defend her character after the murder, because while the act was despicable, she couldn't be an evil person. Her résumé showed as much. She was like them. So it must've been something out of her control, right?

No. "Other moms do not need to worry that they're just going to 'snap' and attack their children," the professor said. "The truth is, there's a backstory to this, a lead-up to this. We are always becoming something, even if it's not obvious to others on the outside."

Sure enough, as we learned more about the story, he was right. There had been warning signs over the years, but her public goodness, her outward appearance, allowed them to go tragically unchecked.

It's good news that we don't snap. The bad news is that our character, if we seem externally like "good people," can become horribly disfigured without us, or anyone else, realizing it. Those of us who don't murder anyone may still be darkly embittered, selfish, and hateful inside without knowing it.

Jesus keeps alerting us to this. He's after our hearts, not a publicly clean rap sheet: "You have heard that it was said to the people long ago, 'You shall not murder, and anyone who murders will be subject to judgment.' But I tell you that anyone who is angry with a brother or sister will be subject to judgment" (Matt. 5:21–22).

Then he does it again with another of the Ten Commandments—the one about adultery. So, you haven't actually committed adultery? Great, but it doesn't make you a good person: "You have heard that it was said, 'You shall not commit adultery.' But I tell you that anyone who looks at a woman lustfully has already committed adultery with her in his heart" (vv. 27–28).

This should be a deathblow to our "at least I'm not like one of those evil people" stories, but our self-stories have a daunting power over us.

Nobody Is Drago

My friend Sherri says, "We all think we're Rocky." We all think we're the hero underdog. I think she's onto something.

In Rocky terms, all of us see ourselves running in Philadelphia, raising our arms to the sky, taking on the world. We're the ones scratching and clawing to heroically make our way through life against all odds. Others try to get in our way, but we will fight the good fight, somehow, someway.

There we are, all of us en masse, climbing the stairs at the Art Museum in our sweats. All of us jogging in place, looking out over the cold city. All of us hearing the music.

We're all gonna fly now.

But, you'll notice, absolutely nobody sees himself as the evil opponent, Russian boxer Ivan Drago. "Me? I am the bad guy with all the advantages. I'm hooked up to these awesome advanced machines while I run on this treadmill because I want to destroy the feel-good story of the year. That's me. I get all the breaks."

Here's a major problem with this, beyond the fact that there just can't be seven billion Italian Stallions: This self-concept allows us to justify anything in the service of our heroic stories. No matter what we do, we can come up with a defense. I'm the hero, the good guy, you know?

As we've seen, our justifications are custom-made and ingenious. They have to be, because they're constructed to fool ourselves. As Guy Swanson writes in *Ego Defenses and the Legitimization of Behavior*, the defenses are "so designed that the defender, not just other people, can accept them."[2]

I'm guessing Darren Armstrong would agree with that. He spoke to a writer for Vice.com about how he used to attack people and rob them, and how he justified all of it in his mind. He says he "felt the system had let me down." And besides, he told himself, he was fighting for fairness. He'd see someone and ask, "Why should he have nice stuff when I've got nothing?"[3]

In the same article, other criminals detail the ways they convinced themselves they were in the right. A man jailed for attempted murder (and who now works as an addictions counselor) says he "justified my wrongdoing to everyone, including myself."[4]

Another man justified his years of crime by putting himself in the role of the hero, an underdog making his way through a difficult world by being successful and skilled at what he did to people. "My justifications involved [blaming] corrupt politicians, police, and society."[5]

Paul, writing in Romans, says there's only one real justification for sinners like me. Big relief: Someone else provided it, and it's all we need.

> For all have sinned and fall short of the glory of God, and all are justified freely by his grace through the redemption that came by Christ Jesus. God presented Christ as a sacrifice of atonement, through the shedding of his blood—to be received by faith. He did this to demonstrate his righteousness, because in his forbearance he had left the sins committed beforehand unpunished—he did it to demonstrate his righteousness at the present time, so as to be just and the one who justifies those who have faith in Jesus. (Rom. 3:23–26)

I can know I'm valuable without having to prove my goodness.

Honestly, that Scripture is something I've had to read several times. It's confusing at first, at least to me. But if I believe it to be true, I don't need to play the justify-myself game anymore. I can know I'm valuable without having to prove my goodness. I don't rewrite reality to fit myself into the role of Rocky, the good guy. I get to be less defensive. I

142

don't need to concoct any more cover stories to fool others or myself.

The pressure's off.

I have a friend who's a counselor, and he told me about some of his clients who are athletes. They have the "yips," he says. Apparently, there's a phenomenon where they can have a mental block and what was once routine becomes incredibly difficult. A pro golfer suddenly can't putt straight. A second baseman can't throw to first base. A basketball player airballs his free throws.

Insightfully, I asked, "So what? After all, I have made something of a lifestyle of airballing free throws. It's kind of a signature move."

He replied, "Yeah, but you're terrible. This guy was a four-star recruit known for being a pure shooter."

"So what's going on when they suddenly can't do basic things?"

"The bottom line is it's too much pressure," he said. "It becomes bigger than a free throw. There's more at stake than there needs to be. It's like, 'If I don't perform well, I've got no identity. I have no reason for my existence. I have no justification.' At some level, they feel like life is hanging in the balance, and they have to prove to someone that they really matter. And then everything and everyone becomes a threat. The crowd, the announcers, the coaches—everybody. So I feel like my job is to help people realize they don't really need to be successful at this in order to have an identity or be loved."

It makes a kind of weird sense. If everything is riding on this thing I'm doing, the "yips" are understandable. There's just so very much at stake.

The Opinion That Matters

Speaking of athletes and fighters and such, I just watched an interview with Jon Jones, who's a UFC champion. He was talking with the interviewer, Joe Rogan, about taking criticism for his personal life.

Jones: Everybody feels like they have the right to tell me to get my [stuff] together. But you know how many [bad people] there are in the world. So many people are into some crazy [stuff].

Rogan: Yeah, but you can't compare yourself to the losers of the losers. I know what you're talking about, like you can say, "Hey, like compared to dudes who like to . . . , I'm fine."

Jones: Exactly. Who knows what weird [stuff] this guy's in and he's telling me to get my [stuff] together. But just because my [stuff] is public don't mean you're any better than I am.

Rogan: That's true, but you know what? That conflict is never ending and you can't get involved in it. That conflict that you're starting up in your brain right now, it's a rationalization conflict. You start rationalizing your behavior versus, "Well, a lot of other people do worse, a lot of other people . . ." Well, that's a dead end. That's a bad road that a lot of people go down to make themselves feel better.

Jones: Right.

Rogan: The only thing that can make you feel better is to be pure, or to be clean. Because if someone comes up to me and says, "Hey, man, you been ripping off old ladies and stealing money from the church," I'd be like, 'What the [heck] are you talking about?" That doesn't make any sense. It's not true at all.

So if someone says something to you that's rude that's not true, it doesn't have any impact on you. But if someone says something that's rude but true, then you have to rationalize, then you have to be like, "Well, what about *you*, man? What's going on with *your* life? Maybe *you* are into some dark [stuff], you know."

That's a bad road. It's a defensive road. . . . That is a trap, man, that is a trap.[6]

Exactly. It's a trap, and Rogan makes a brilliant point. Still, I'd argue we're in trouble if we have to be "pure" on the basis of our own goodness. What about when we're actually guilty of things? Things we can't undo? That's all of us. How do we start over?

And what if the voice making the accusations about you . . . is you? What if you're the one who's brutal on yourself? What if you are overrun with regret, and it's based on failings that are very real? (I'm asking for a friend.)

Honestly, this is something I've struggled with my whole life. I can obsess over my failures, how I blew this opportunity or that one, how I forgot to return that email, or how I've let people down. Something dumb or unfair or hurtful I said ten years ago can suddenly pop into my memory, and it feels like a punch to the gut.

Maybe you can relate to this. Or maybe you'll think I'm a weirdo. Or maybe both, which is perfectly reasonable.

It's remarkable how I can vacillate from self-incrimination to self-righteousness. Maybe I don't even vacillate. Maybe it's simultaneous. Maybe the self-incrimination and self-righteousness feed each other.

As we've seen, there are a lot of options for how to deal with this guilt. We can compare ourselves with "worse" people. Change our fundamental belief systems to fit what we're doing. Blame others. Become more fervently moralistic in other areas. Rationalize and justify.

But another option is to actually believe God really did forgive me, and that what happened on the cross really matters. If God, who knows me and my motives better than I know myself, has elected to forgive me, and if I'm really going to submit to him, then I have to forgive myself too.

What he did to cover my sin has to matter. His opinion of me has to outweigh mine.

FOURTEEN

A Short Chapter about the Previous Chapter

Some Ideas to Address Our Drive to Self-Justify

In light of my capacity to justify my actions in my own head, here are some strategies I've learned to try to avoid them. When I use them, I'm spared a lot of silly, internal story writing, excuse making, and needless anger. They might be helpful for you too.

I try to see everybody *else* as Rocky.

There's an old saying, and we're not quite sure who said it first, but it goes something like this: "Be kind, for everyone you meet is fighting a hard battle."

So much of the essence of love is simply rooting for people. I want to know what people are really up against, even if they don't know it themselves, and see the beauty in them, even if they don't see that in themselves.

I get the impression this is what Jesus did, and this is the reason his public reproaches were so passionate. He genuinely wanted people to turn around so they could be what they were meant to be. There really are great stories waiting to happen for them, if only they would somehow humble themselves.

Maybe everybody else is Rocky, and I'm Apollo Creed. He's kind of a jerk, but eventually he winds up backing Rocky and even training him. He wants someone else to win. (I know I'm milking this Rocky thing, but I'm really enjoying it.)

I try to let my ego's story drop away.

I get these daily emails for people with my personality type on the Enneagram. (My official personality type is "Awkward Nerd Guy.") One day the email reminded me that "growth does not come from gaining more and more knowledge. Growth comes from allowing your ego's story to drop away."

I like that. I need to allow my "ego's story to drop away." Well put, email-writer person.

As we've discussed, we're all operating under certain self-written stories. Sometimes we're not even aware of what they are. But so often they're all about protecting our ego. Life is better when I am conscious of being less defensive.

I remember how *good* God is.

I'm notoriously forgetful. Sure, I've stored away libraries of knowledge to win on trivia night, but every single day,

I lose things. It's actually kind of fun for me. Every new morning is a treasure hunt: for my keys, for my phone, for my car.

Thankfully, it's not just me. Everyone is very, very forgetful. The Israelites were rescued via unspeakably dramatic miracles . . . and forgot about them within hours. God told his people to write things on doorposts, to wrap reminders around their wrists, so they'd remember that they are his people and he is their God.

> When I get self-obsessed, anxious, or defensive, honestly, I need to be reminded of how faithful God has been to me.

We're just really forgetful, so we default back to "it's about me." We know better, but we need to be reminded.

When I get self-obsessed, anxious, or defensive, honestly, I need to be reminded of how faithful God has been to me. There's something about his kindness that turns me around, sure, but I have to remember it.

And when I bother to think about it . . . *he's been very, very good*. I need that to be top-of-mind more.

God is actually *for* us. He really is.

Remembering this can take the pressure off. Instead of defaulting to protecting my ego story, I can relax and be far less defensive. He's my defender.

I try not to say, "At least I don't . . ."

Someone else sins differently than I do, so somehow I'm not so bad? Really? Yes, it's a classic maneuver, this "at least I don't . . ." evasion. It's also shallow, weak, and childish.

I want to drop anger and instead extend forgiveness to others as it's been extended to me.

My self-righteousness produces anger; it doesn't mitigate it. As I argued in *Unoffendable* (very convincingly, I think), the Bible knows nothing of human "righteous anger." We made that up. God's anger is righteous; ours isn't. We're told to get rid of it before the sun goes down.

"Anger indulged, instead of simply waved off, always has in it an element of self-righteousness and vanity," Dallas Willard wrote. "Find a person who has embraced anger, and you find a person with a wounded ego."[1]

We certainly may not enjoy what someone has done to us, but we do, at a certain level, enjoy being angry. This is because it feeds our sense of rightness in comparison to what the other person did.

People who believe their anger is righteous aren't sure how long they're supposed to hold on to it. Forever? So the anger must be continually justified. Stories have to be retold, at least to ourselves, and our relationships are permanently destroyed.

"But Jesus got angry! He cleared out the temple!"

Well, yes, he did. But he is sinless, and we're not. Like my friend Sherri says (she says a lot of great stuff), "No, sweetheart, you don't get a whip. You're the money changer."

I need to remember I'm a terrible judge.

Another well-known cognitive bias is called the *actor-observer bias*. It's simply this: We see our own behavior as caused by external circumstances. We see others' behavior as due to their own internal decisions.

We're both grumpy? Well, that's because the dog woke me up too early this morning, plus I just got an unfair parking ticket. But you're grumpy because you're being a jerk.

We both flunked an algebra test? Well, my sister was being loud so I couldn't study last night, plus the questions weren't quite clear. You failed it because maybe you're just not smart enough.

I fail because of other stuff. You fail because of you. That's how this works.

We don't see others' circumstances, and we don't see ourselves clearly either. I'm a bad judge of you and a bad judge of me. When I'm aware of this, I spend less energy defending myself and less time trying to justify everything I do.

I try to trust God more.

The tax collector in Jesus' story did something seldom seen: He completely gave up on his own righteousness. He was a disaster, he admitted it, and he threw himself on God's mercy. All he had was a seven-word prayer that acknowledged reality.

That's it. Seven words. Jesus wants us to be like that guy.

Struggle as we might, fail as we might, doubt as we might—it's not *our* strength that can rescue us. We may as well admit it.

In Mark Helprin's magnificent novel *A Soldier of the Great War*, two prisoners face imminent execution. Alessandro is a very flawed man who believes in God's goodness, and Ludovico is an atheist and Marxist revolutionary. To explain his faith in God despite his own failings and doubts, Alessandro recalls his high-speed jumps on his beloved horse over high fences with spikes near his home:

"Would you have trusted the horse to carry you over the spikes, time and time again, and not be impaled?" he asked. Ludovico said no. "Yes," Alessandro continued. "It was dangerous, irrational, the fence was far too high. Even when I approached the barrier, I myself did not truly believe that he could take me over."

"So why did you do it?"

"I trusted his strength and goodness more than I believe my weakness and my doubt. It always worked. It was a good lesson."[2]

I want to remember there's hope. God is changing me.

We really can become less intent on justifying ourselves. We *can* become more aware of our brokenness and less judgmental of others. John Ortberg writes about some heartening research in his book *Soul Keeping*:

In a study conducted in Beijing, researchers compared which part of the brain people used to evaluate both themselves and others. The study is summarized in an article with the snappy title, "Neural Consequences of Religious Belief on Self-Referential Processing." Non-religious subjects used one part of the brain (the ventral medial prefrontal cortex, in case you're interested) to evaluate themselves, but another part (the dorsal medial prefrontal cortex) to evaluate others. Christians used the same part of the brain to evaluate themselves that they used to evaluate others. Researchers hypothesized this is because they were actually using a kind of "Jesus reference point" for self-evaluation; they were really asking, "What does God think of me?" UCLA researcher Jeff Schwartz said that this study is one of the most important scientific papers published in the last decade. Prayer, meditation, and confession actually have the power to rewire the brain in a way that can make us less self-referential and more aware of how God sees us.[3]

I like that. We can change and become "more aware of how God sees us."

And how God sees us, my reader friend, is great news. The most important being in the universe knows you better than you know yourself, and still finds you worthy of paying the highest price.

No further justifications are needed.

FIFTEEN

How to Get Kicked Out of the Church of Satan

Battling Self-Righteousness by Loving Your
Enemy as Much as Yourself

> Check me out: I'm totally quoting myself in my chapter about
> loving ourselves.
>
> —Brant Hansen

The other day, I sat in a terribly boring meeting. It went on
for hours. I couldn't stay awake. But then it got exciting, because . . . the subject changed to me, Brant P. Hansen. I was
suddenly alert and engaged. I was dialed in. This is because
I've always been interested in the subject of me. It doesn't
sound modest. But it's true.

Is it normal? I think so, but it's still embarrassing that if
I was honestly filling out an interest survey, I would include

puppetry, stamps, and me, Brant Hansen. And The Lord of the Rings. And toast.

But definitely also me.

The Love/Hate Relationship

Here's the part where I expand on how I actually don't like myself very much, because that's true too.

Inwardly, I've always struggled to stop berating myself. I question every move I make. I get frustrated with my own habits of mind, my own ways of saying things. I get sick of my own voice. I greatly dislike how my once-broken nose slopes to one side. I often cringe, after the fact, at my own awkwardness. I'm aware I've used the word "I" seven times already in this paragraph. I better make that ten. Eleven.

In my innermost thoughts, I have a common name for myself, and I'm embarrassed by this, but here we go. It's "idiot." When I mess something up, when I lose my laptop, when I forget an appointment, when I say something stupid, that's the word that pops into my head. *You IDIOT.*

If someone else loses a laptop, I don't call them an idiot. If they miss an appointment with me, I don't call them an idiot. I don't even think it. But I say it to myself.

What's more, as I've mentioned, even when I'm not aggravated by dumb things I'm currently doing, I can sit and roil with regret on demand. Like an unspooling film, memories of me doing the wrong things cascade onto the floor. And the hits keep coming. Things I've said at just the wrong time, thoughtless things I've done, selfish decisions I've made . . .

Since I'm a syndicated radio personality, I'll occasionally be in a car somewhere and unexpectedly hear my voice pop onto the air on some station, and I can't shut it off fast enough. It doesn't matter if I'm sitting in the back. If the people in front won't turn it off or block me from leaping over their seat, I will open the back door at full speed and, Indiana Jones–style, leap over the top of the car onto the hood and reach around through the driver's window to shut the radio off. I hate hearing me.

> I *love* me, and I'm pretty sure I don't *like* me. It's both/and.

So I *love* me, and I'm pretty sure I don't *like* me. It's both/and.

Maybe you don't like hearing yourself either. Maybe you, too, castigate yourself for things you did ten years ago. Maybe you're not thrilled with your personal appearance. Maybe you don't like your voice when you hear a recording. Maybe you call yourself names.

Or—here's another possibility—maybe you just read all the stuff I wrote about me and your takeaway is, "Sheesh. He's right. He really *is* an idiot."

I doubt it. I'm guessing you can relate to me. We humans are quite a paradox. We're both fascinated and frustrated by ourselves. In either case, the late novelist David Foster Wallace agrees that we all struggle with this. "We rarely talk about this sort of natural, basic self-centeredness, because it's so socially repulsive, but it's pretty much the same for all of us, deep down. It is our default-setting, hard-wired into our boards at birth."[1]

Right. We rarely talk about it. Sure, I started this chapter talking about how self-interested I am, but quickly abandoned that direction in favor of the second part, where I got to tell you how much I don't like me.

> Jesus knows we're fighting a daily battle against our default, self-centered nature.

It *is* socially repulsive, this acknowledgment of our self-centeredness, because it reveals the truth about us. And yet, this is a *shared* self-centeredness. It's not just you or just me. This isn't something that should scandalize anyone when we have the audacity to admit it. We're all fighting it.

So when Jesus says we have to deny ourselves each day, he means it, and not just for a select few really bad people. He knows we're fighting a daily battle against our default, self-centered nature.

We get defensive about it and don't want to believe it. We're much more comfortable telling ourselves, and others, that we struggle to love ourselves. "I must learn to love myself first," we say. Or "I can't love others until I love me."

We quote Jesus on this, from the greatest commandment, in which he tells us, "Love the Lord your God with all your heart and with all your soul and with all your mind and with all your strength. . . . Love your neighbor as yourself" (Mark 12:30–31). And our takeaway is somehow, "I need to learn to love myself."

I'm not so sure that's an emphasis at all in what Jesus is saying. Even if we don't like ourselves too much, we seem to already love ourselves quite easily.

I Must Love This Guy

I'll give you an example of love in action. This is something I don't talk about much, but for years I have been the principal caregiver for an adult man. Honestly, he frequently smells. He has to be fed. He makes messes. He needs his teeth brushed. And, in even grosser news, he needs to be cleaned up after using the restroom. I do all of this for him.

When he gets sick, I pray for him. I take him to the doctor and make sure he takes his pills. I can't stand it when he's in pain. It really hurts me. Plus I root for him. I want him to succeed. He used to play baseball, and even though he was terrible, guess which team I always pulled for? His.

I drive him to work. I want him to get the respect he deserves, and it bothers me when he doesn't. It bugs me when people put him down or take credit for something he did.

I spend a good portion of my income to house him. I buy his clothes and try to get things that look good on him. I want people to think he looks nice. I even take him to the gym.

I take care of his basics and have provided for his entertainment. Even though he goofs off a lot, I make sure he has a computer and smartphone to help him be productive. I was elated when I was finally able to give him a car he liked, one that wouldn't break down every few miles.

And, as I mentioned, when he's the subject of a long, boring meeting, I suddenly wake up and pay attention.

Wow, I must love that guy, right? I mean, he drives me crazy, sure, but to do all that, I must love him.

Jesus seems to take this for granted, in fact, that we already love ourselves. *He's telling us to love our neighbors in the same way.* What if they're in pain and can't find help? What if they need a place to stay? What if they could use a ride to work? Love them, he says, like . . . like . . . well, like you love you.

Jesus doesn't say we shouldn't love ourselves. He just doesn't spend much time on it. He wants our love for ourselves under his authority, where it won't become something both grotesque and deadly. He argues for a life of servanthood and forgiveness that forces our self-love into something humble and freeing.

Humility isn't self-denigration. My longtime struggle with a self-incriminating, inner dialogue is not born of humility. Our frustration with who we are or where we are in life is not a sign of humility. As Rick Warren famously wrote, "Humility is not thinking less of yourself, it's thinking of yourself less."[2]

Humility is realizing that we are not the authority, then submitting to the real authority.

This authority issue is so central that followers of Jesus were told to believe and publicly say, "Jesus is Lord." That means not Caesar and not one of us. Anyone else in apparent "authority" merely serves at the King's pleasure . . . and only for now.

"All of us, like sheep, have strayed away," Isaiah says. "We have left God's paths to follow our own" (53:6 NLT).

Notice how it's our *own* path. It's not obviously evil. It's not marked "This Is the Evil Path" or "Satan Boulevard." In my case, it's just "Brant Hansen's Self-Righteous Way."

By the way, *Satan* means "adversary" or "accuser" in the Hebrew of the Old Testament. But the word comes loaded with common images, most of which came centuries after the Bible was written and were based on pagan perceptions of what demons might look like.

As cartoonish as some of those images may be, the fact that a real spiritual adversary exists is a given to Jesus. In Scripture, Jesus talks about and interacts with the adversary. It's part of the biblical story early on. Apparently, some spiritual beings misused their free will, and like most petulant, doomed losers, they want to take others down with them. According to the Bible, their primary modus operandi isn't drawing us into Satan worship. It's cheering us on as we put ourselves in authority. It's imploring us to chart our own paths, to believe in our own "goodness," and to reject the authority of the real King.

Modern Satanists agree with me here. "Satanism is not Devil-worship. No matter how often we restate this, misunderstandings persist," the Church of Satan website says. "After all, the mythological Satan doesn't worship any gods above Himself. Neither do we. Every Satanist is his or her own god. You can't get more Satanic than that!"[3]

(By the way, here's a free Pro Tip for the Church of Satan: If you don't want "misunderstandings" to persist that you worship Satan, maybe don't call it the "Church of Satan." Just throwing that out there.)

We love to pat ourselves on the back for being good. "It's not like I'm *evil*, doing weird stuff like joining a coven or something." But dark, dress-up rituals have never been the goal of the adversary as described in the Bible. His goal is to deny the authority of Christ, to reject the kingship of Jesus.

So, if you ever want to get your membership yanked from the Church of Satan, here are some ideas:

1. Acknowledge you're not your own god. This shouldn't be so difficult for me, as not only am I not all-knowing, but I sometimes lose my car in the parking lot. Not because I can't remember where I parked it, but because I can't remember what my car looks like.

2. Believe that Jesus, and no one else, is Lord. He's the authority.
3. Love your enemies.

That should do it. That will get you booted from the potluck supper. You will not be invited to be part of the Church of Satan Greeters Ministry or the Connections Luncheon.

Jesus Is #3

It so happens that "love your enemies" was apparently one of the most popular, oft-repeated things Jesus said among early believers. Writer Preston Sprinkle notes, "It was quoted in 26 places by 10 different writers in the first 300 years of Christianity, which makes it *the* most celebrated command among the first Christians."[4]

I don't think it's been celebrated much since then.

There's a book called *The 100: A Ranking of the Most Influential Persons in History*. When I found it, I knew it would be arbitrary, but I like rankings and lists. I wondered where Jesus would finish. I opened it up.

Jesus finishes at #3.

Muhammed gets the #1 seed, and Isaac Newton checks in right behind him.[5] (Personal disappointment: The inventor of toast is nowhere on the list.)

Now, to be sure, billions of humans, including me, have believed that Jesus rose from the dead. He's also the central flashpoint of history. We even date things according to his life. In my opinion, that trumps Newton's contributions to physics, and even his pioneering work in fig-based snack cookies.

The author of *The 100* said he *would* have given Jesus the top spot but for one of Jesus' teachings, both breathtaking and scandalous: "Love your enemies." If that one had caught on, he wrote, well, Jesus would've been #1, no problem. But it didn't.

The author has a fair point. It's been 2,000-plus years, and if aliens landed on earth, I doubt they'd look at our history and say, "You know what you guys are really good at? Loving your enemies. Now, let us help you with your overpriced coffee issue."

It's tragic, because loving our enemies is an antidote to the poison of self-righteousness. It requires a renovated heart. It requires obedience. It's an act of worship before God. It puts our self-love in a healthy place—under his kingship. And yes, it's a struggle to love our enemies, but it's a heroic one.

Loving ourselves? We're naturals at that.

Loving our enemies? Wanting them to flourish in spite of themselves? Now we're talking about something glorious.

Something that's less like me and more like Jesus.

SIXTEEN

Even More Good News: The Humble Life Is More Fun Anyway

Battling Self-Righteousness by Becoming Childlike

> The secret of life lies in laughter and humility.
>
> —G. K. Chesterton

This whole book has been about humility, of course. I thought about titling it *Seriously, You Guys: We Need to Humble Ourselves and Stop Being Big, Self-Obsessed Dumbheads*, but I'm told by "publishing experts" that people don't actually want to buy that book. Then I thought about titling it *Publishing Experts: The REAL Dumbheads*, and that didn't go over so great either.

But, my goodness, humility is a wondrous thing. Like Chesterton says, it's the secret of life, along with laughter, and those things go together naturally.

Jesus tells us to become like children if we want to enter the kingdom of heaven. It so happens that kids are the undisputed champs of laughter. Perhaps you've seen the stats that show they laugh ten times more per day than adults do, and while I can't find reliable research on it, it seems to jibe with my observation.

At the time of this writing, there's a particular high-profile politician on the world stage who's known for his lack of humility. I hadn't noticed this, but a longtime associate of his mentioned something about him: You'll never catch him laughing. He doesn't laugh.

> The smallest, silliest, most repetitive things can be delightful when you don't fancy yourself in charge of everything.

To be fair, responsibility can weigh a person down. But that's just the point. The more we can trust God with our world, the less weight we're under and the more we can laugh.

When you're a kid, you have no responsibilities, really, so the smallest things can be funny. I remember playing a "secret word" game with my son when he was tiny. I'd tell him not a say a particular silly word (it's a secret, or I'd tell you). Of course, he'd say it over and over and I'd act aggravated and start tickling him. We did this exactly 47,000 times. The smallest, silliest, most repetitive things can be delightful when you don't fancy yourself in charge of everything.

Kids don't seem terribly interested in crafting a public persona. No, that's a thing older people do. We grown-ups are very interested in controlling people's perceptions of us. It's a burden. Like we noted earlier in the book, we act as our own PR person, our own spokesperson, and it's exhausting to always be spinning things to our advantage.

Jesus said we'd have to become like children to enter the kingdom, because children know they're not in control of everything. They're not anxious about tomorrow. They're in the moment. If there's a God and he really loves us, well, it makes sense that he'd want us to be like that. He'd want us to laugh. He'd want us to admit who we really are. No wonder Jesus told us to get over ourselves and turn toward him.

He really did say that, by the way. In a hundred ways. He said, too, that he wants us to have life, and have it to the full (see John 10:10). He told us that if we lose our own lives for his sake, we'll find real life (see Matt. 16:25).

It's a startling message, and it's ironic when we treat it lightly.

I think about how most people in the US believe in ETI—extraterrestrial intelligence. There are those who long for contact with more advanced species from outer space and hope that they will bring us wisdom to help us save ourselves. It's the basis not only of the SETI (search for extraterrestrial intelligence) program, but also of thousands of sci-fi novels, movies, and hopeful discussions among UFO enthusiasts.

What message would a wise being bring from another place? After millennia of violence, division, and even carnage, we need outside help! We await this enlightenment!

In the story of Jesus, we have an advanced life form. He is wisdom and love in the form of a man who delivers himself to us. And his message, put very roughly, is (drum-roll, please) . . .

"I love you. And seriously, you are sick. Get over your-selves. You are sheep. You need me."

Sheep? Us?

And so the search continues. *Anybody else out there?*

Real Humility

Yes, the truth about us really is the Good News—that God still wants us, and he is restoring the world. He'll even use us to do it. We're not good people, but we're deeply loved anyway. And the truth about us is like all truth from Jesus: It sets us free, in so many unexpected and profound ways.

I've got a long way to go on this humility thing. I know that. But I'm glad I can look back and see some growth, however gradual. Things that years ago would have left me angry or aggravated for days are no longer so threatening.

This is a good thing for anyone, but it's especially helpful for a guy whose work is so public. For example, I just bought a coffee before sitting down to write this chapter. The barista (who's a very nice lady) happens to know I'm the goofy guy she listens to on the radio. As she took my order, she told me she'd heard the new song I'd written and performed with my guitar on the show yesterday.

I'm not always good at reading humans, but I think her view of my artistic effort was, on balance, largely negative. The reason I got that impression is because she said it was—quoting here—"absolutely horrible." Another indicator was when she asked me to please not write any more songs. She said the word "horrible" a few more times as she handed me my receipt.

And that's okay. I'm honored she listens to the show. Or "listened"? I'm honored she used to listen. She really is a nice lady. And the song may actually have been horrible.

Then I got a tweet from someone I don't know: "Dude, you are the worst. Every time you come on the radio, I want to plow my Jeep into a tree."

This sort of criticism used to make me want to purchase my own Jeep just so I could plow it into a tree. But now I'm amused. I even applaud his descriptiveness. He could have just said I was horrible, but he elaborated so colorfully.

I'm convinced my pride is the great destroyer of everything fun, and I'm much more fun to be around when I can get over myself.

It's our pride that drives us from God. Nothing else can do it. "Neither death nor life, neither angels nor demons," Paul writes to believers in Rome, "neither our fears for today nor our worries about tomorrow—not even the powers of hell can separate us from God's love" (Rom. 8:38 NLT).

All the forces of the universe cannot stop us . . . *if* we finally come to the end of ourselves. No one can truly harm us . . . *if* we allow God to be our defender.

True humility is the final repudiation of self-righteousness, the rejection of the very idea that our way is better, that somehow we'd be more, accomplish more, or reach our potential if we rejected God's way for our own.

Again, I turn to the late novelist David Foster Wallace's phrasing of our problem, when he gave a speech to graduating students about how our culture is all about worship of self and our own personal freedom: "The freedom all to be lords of our tiny skull-sized kingdoms, alone at the center of creation."[1]

"Lord of the Tiny Skull-Sized Kingdom" is not something

I aspire to, even if it does sound kind of Lord-of-the-Rings-y. Sadly, it really is the endpoint of our self-righteous trajectory, "alone at the center of creation."

I've been thinking about this for the last couple months, after we got our golden retriever puppy. She's a great dog. Her name is Cozy. We had to get her a little halter for her walks, because we couldn't do the usual leash-collar arrangement. She would choke herself. Over and over, Cozy would pull to where she wanted to go and ultimately make herself miserable. Again and again.

Dogs are weird that way, huh? I mean, why don't they quit doing dumb things and hurting themselves? Odd little creatures.

I'm her master and I love her, and I have big plans for her. She just needs to follow my lead. It takes time and it's frustrating, but I have a vision for the future: It's us heading to the beach for long summer days. Jogging. Swimming. And it's us setting out from our house for daylong, meandering adventures. We'll explore together!

I can't wait. Games of fetch in the sand! Frisbee! Long, happy runs together in the Florida sun. Oh, the places we will go! She's going to love it! It's just a matter of time and a matter of trust. It's going to be beautiful. She just doesn't know it yet.

Her master has big plans, indeed, and once she learns to quit pulling her own way, she's in for a world of freedom.

Baby Bear Indignation

There's an added, rarely talked-about benefit to doing away with our self-righteousness once and for all: *It keeps us from ruining everything all the time.*

No, really. Everything. All the time. Have you noticed how when we're on a self-righteous kick (and the "kick" can last our whole lives), we can't just let a thing be a thing? We're looking for ways to make the thing into an opportunity to teach others a lesson, to be offended, or to show how enlightened we are. In other words, to ruin everything.

I was reminded of this today when I saw a video of some baby bears playing together. Somebody got mad about it.

The bears snuck into a backyard in Colorado and jumped in a pool. They were playing with the pool toys, including a noodle ($2.96 at Walmart) and an inflatable mattress ($2 at Dollar General.) It was a delightful video. Of course, I'm biased in favor of baby bears playing, because I'm generally for babies, bears, and playing.

But then the inevitable comments: "This is an outrage that some of you find this amusing. These bears are destroying someone's property, and shame on you all for encouraging this." And so forth.

Yes, of course. Someone is against baby bears playing. There's something about self-righteousness that kills the fun every time. It makes us want to teach people instead of just enjoying a moment.

> There's something about self-righteousness that kills the fun every time.

It happens to otherwise great movies sometimes. What was a lighthearted, fun comedy suddenly tries to teach us something. It can't just be funny. We can't merely enjoy ourselves, because for the self-righteous, laughter is never enough.

I read a review of *Incredibles 2*, and the critic found the movie funny but faulted it for being insufficiently important.

It didn't teach us anything about current issues and events. It had no overarching point about society. It didn't lecture us. Sure, we laughed, but the movie didn't grapple with the weighty issues.

But I'm grateful to the makers of *Incredibles 2* for not grappling with the weighty issues. I'm not sure we always need to be taught about the weighty issues. They're burdensome—hence the term *weighty*, I guess—and I can't bear them all the time.

Self-righteousness means bearing weighty issues all the time. In fact, this is exactly the language Jesus uses about self-righteous people: "They tie up heavy, cumbersome loads and put them on other people's shoulders, but they themselves are not willing to lift a finger to move them" (Matt. 23:4).

Self-righteousness puts us under a heavy weight, but it doesn't stop there. It also makes us think our job is to help everyone else feel the weight. When we are drawn to the way of Jesus, we start doing the opposite: lifting burdens from the backs of others. We make it a habit. We don't put up barricades. We welcome people, even other people like us.

In what will be the least surprising revelation of this book, I need to tell you that I was an oddball growing up. Even so, I was once invited to a popular girl's birthday party. Her parents had enough money to take a lot of kids to the fair. We got free rides all evening long.

To this day, I don't know how I got on the guest list. Being a kid, I had the good sense not to question it. I just enjoyed the rides. I was too relieved and happy.

Relief + happiness = lots of laughter and fun. After all, we've been found out. We deserve punishment, and instead,

God invites us to his great feast. Sure, it feels like there was some mistake with the invite list—how did *we* get in here? But since we're standing here enjoying this ridiculously awesome party, well . . . don't say anything about it when some other unqualified losers come in. Just smile and nod, my friend.

By the way, I just finished reading *A Gentleman in Moscow*. It's a novel about a young Russian aristocrat found guilty of insufficiently supporting the Communist party after the revolution. He's sentenced to live out the remainder of his life in the confines of a hotel. He spends decades as a waiter. He makes friends with others who've had to come to grips with their new status, and he enjoys them. He calls them the "Confederacy of the Humbled":

> Like the Freemasons, the Confederacy of the Humbled is a close-knit brotherhood whose members travel with no outward markings, but who know each other at a glance. For having fallen suddenly from grace, those in the Confederacy share a certain perspective. Knowing beauty, influence, fame, and privilege to be borrowed rather than bestowed, they are not easily impressed. They are not quick to envy or take offense. They certainly do not scour the papers in search of their own names. They remain committed to living among their peers, but they greet adulation with caution, ambition with sympathy, and condescension with an inward smile.[2]

I love it. I want to live this way.

I know when it comes to church names, we apparently prefer things like "First Baptist" or "Crossroads Community" or that sort of thing, but honestly, if anyone starts a church called the "Confederacy of the Humbled," I'm joining.

The Right Hand

I remember being a little kid in a crowd. I was three, maybe four, years old. It was after an outdoor play in a small town in Kentucky. The play was over, there was applause, and everyone turned to grab their keys and purses and programs. I grabbed my mom's hand so she could lead me through the confusing gathering of hundreds on our way to the car.

I still remember the odd feeling—something like vertigo—when I heard a woman's voice above me: "Honey, I'm not your mom."

I looked up, and sure enough, it was another lady, still holding my hand. Where was my mom? Who was this woman? She smiled at me, but I felt like I was free-falling. It was complete disorientation. Reality itself seemed up for grabs. The lady quickly and kindly led me through the crowd until she found my mom. My mom thanked her profusely, I grabbed my mom's hand, and the universe was rightly ordered again.

I feel sometimes like we're all doing this. Like we're all grabbing the wrong hand and then trying to make ourselves think it's not so. I think we've forgotten who we are because we've forgotten whose we are.

If the truth about us comes as an unwelcome surprise at first, it leads us to the greatest news in the history of the universe: We can know who we are. We can trust God with the weighty issues. We can be his children again.

That means more laughing. Count me in.

SEVENTEEN

The Final Chapter: The One Where I Finally Mention Kermit

Enjoying the Freedom of Humility

> May your expectations all be frustrated, may all of your plans be thwarted, may all of your desires be withered into nothingness, that you may experience the powerlessness and poverty of a child and can sing and dance in the love of God the Father, Son and Holy Spirit.
>
> —John Ortberg

There's a great scene in the 1980s film *The Mission* where Robert De Niro's character bears a literal heavy weight up a waterfall to make himself pay—unnecessarily—for his sins. It's an unforgettably stirring scene, and I won't ruin it for you.

Rarely do we get to see such a vivid visual reminder of how most of us go about life. As we've discussed throughout this book, even if we don't want to believe in the idea of sin, or God for that matter, we find ourselves trying to prove our goodness, to somehow justify ourselves, to cross the terrible gap.

In this final chapter, I thought I'd mention just some of the freedoms that come with desperately admitting, "I'm not a good person," finally trusting that God bore the weight for us, and dropping it into the river far below.

Maybe, as you read this, you could add to the list. These are things I'm learning, and this journey's far from over. My instinct continues to be to protect myself, to try to go back to a lifestyle of rationalization, excuse making, confabulating, and pretending that I'm good. But I'm learning to fight that instinct. I'm learning to trust God more.

Getting over my self-righteousness means freedom from confabulating.

When I'm living a life of humility, I'm free to say those three shocking, countercultural words that no one sees coming: "I don't know."

Confabulating means making up a story, and we all do it. (Remember the pantyhose experiment back in chapter 3, when people came up with reasons why their preference was a higher quality than the other samples?) We can't seem to resist holding forth on things we really know nothing about. We want to offer an answer, any answer, or some opinion. But we so often don't know what the heck we're talking about. We just say stuff anyway.

Watch any "Man on the Street" bit on a late night show or YouTube and you'll see it in action. People are asked questions they can't possibly answer, and they'll answer them anyway.

Interviewer: What did you think of the debate last
night? Who do you think won?

Man on the street: Oh, I think [favorite candi-
date] won. He really dominated. It was
great.

Problem: The candidates haven't even debated, yet one
person after another answers the question anyway. They'll
even expand on one of their answers.

Interviewer: Why do you think he won?

Man on the street: I think [favorite candidate]
really made some great points about health
care.

Maybe we're afraid of being caught on video looking
dumb, but I've been practicing this "I don't know" thing
for a while, and I can tell you, it's liberating in the highest
degree.

Not everybody loves when you do this, of course. You're
supposed to act like you know. So I've
gone from being annoying Mr. Know-
It-All to annoying Mr. Apparently-
Doesn't-Know-Anything. But it really
does save time and effort. Just hearing
myself say "I don't know" is strangely
life-giving.

Humility means not having to trick
others, and myself, by making up stories
on the fly.

> I've been
> practicing this "I
> don't know" thing
> for a while, and I
> can tell you, it's
> liberating in the
> highest degree.

Getting over my self-righteousness means freedom to like people more, because I'm criticizing them less.

Believing that I'm not a good person means gossiping less, and that's another beautiful thing.

As we've seen, as I remain aware that I'm not a good person, I become more aware of God's goodness toward me. His love covers me. He covers my shame. This helps me to gossip less and defend others more.

When I don't hear myself going on about what someone else did, when I practice reluctance to complain about others even casually, I'm not stirring up anger within myself. Instead, I'm sacrificing my own desires to serve others. That really is love.

So instead of stoking my self-righteous anger, I'm reversing the process. I'm actually growing in love toward others because that's what happens when I serve someone.

Instead of being trapped, I'm free to see them as God sees them. I'm free to sleep easier at night instead of broiling in my own bitterness.

And this next one is related . . .

Getting over my self-righteousness means freedom from perpetual resentment.

When I really believe I'm not better than anyone else, I cut people slack, which has an almost magical effect on me.

Try this on social media sometime: *When someone says something stupid or wrong or just obnoxious, respond with something genuinely complimentary.* You'll instantly like the person a little more.

It says in Proverbs that "a gentle answer turns away wrath" (15:1). I used to think that meant the other person wouldn't be so wrathful if I was gentle toward them. Now, though, I suspect I'm actually turning away my *own* wrath too. Since the rest of that Proverb says, "but a harsh word stirs up anger," I think it's fair to assume my harsh words stir up my *own* anger too.

I'm far more apt to respond with gentleness when I'm hyper-aware of my own brokenness. My awareness prevents me from living with the resentment that so often accompanies self-righteousness.

Getting over my self-righteousness means freedom from trying to control everybody's reactions.

Self-righteousness is all about controlling perceptions—those of ourselves and others. We self-enhance to convince ourselves we're good, and we work to show everyone else we're good too. It's a never-ending job. Putting an end to the good-person lie frees us from it.

Oddly—and this is a bonus—I've found that not trying to control perceptions makes me someone people are more apt to want to be around.

When I was a kid, my grandparents would watch a show called *The Lawrence Welk Show*, which featured an older gentleman and a series of singers and dancers. It was all very clean and polished. I don't remember much about it except that everyone seemed perfect and there was an accordion player named Myron Floren. He was awesome, and I've downloaded some of his songs, but that's not the point here.

> I've found that not trying to control perceptions makes me someone people are more apt to want to be around.

179

The point is that the show was on Sunday night, and right after it we could flip the channel to another show called *The Muppet Show*. There was an emcee on that too. He was similar to Lawrence Welk, but shorter. And he was a frog. There was also a series of singers and dancers and entertainers, usually chickens and such.

I lived for that show, and it's not just because they had a dog playing piano. It's because the show really wasn't about what was on stage. It was about what was really going on behind the scenes. And behind the scenes, it was kind of a disaster. No one knew who was supposed to go on next. It was disarray and chaos. It was really a show about putting on a show, and that appealed to me greatly.

I'm sure Lawrence Welk was a great guy. He was extremely well groomed. But I know who I still want to hang out with: Kermit.

I want to be like Kermit too, in a way. I want people to see right past whatever it is that I'm trotting onto the public stage. I want them to see the struggle and realize, "Hey, if God is using *that* guy, he can use anybody," because it's true. I don't want to have to carefully manage everyone's perceptions. It was hard even picking an author photo for this book cover. Who wants to do that all the time?

Everyone loves Gonzo on *The Muppet Show*, not because he's excellent but because he's struggling, and we feel like we're right there with him.

"Compassion—which means, literally, 'to suffer with'—is the way to the truth that we are most ourselves, not when we differ from others, but when we are the same," writes Henri Nouwen. "Indeed the main spiritual question is not, 'What difference do you make?' but 'What do you have in common?'

It is not 'excelling' but 'serving' that makes us most human. It is not proving ourselves to be better than others but confessing to be just like others that is the way to healing and reconciliation."[1]

In the kingdom of God, humble servanthood is better than excellence.

And whether you agree or disagree, I think you can respect that I totally just worked Henri Nouwen and Gonzo into the same point.

> In the kingdom of God, humble servanthood is better than excellence.

Getting over my self-righteousness means freedom from trying to control God.

Humility, as we've seen, means acknowledging this once and for all: *God owes me nothing.* He cannot be manipulated. Prayer is not a magic spell that, if I repeat it a certain number of times or do it a certain way, will obligate God to do something. This is not how relationships work. This relationship is about the truth, which is that God is the righteous one, I'm not, and there's no pretending anymore.

I like what N. T. Wright wrote about this, mainly because he used the word *prig*, which is not a dirty word, by the way. I looked it up to make sure. Twice. He said, "Someone who is determinedly trying to show God how good he or she is is likely to become an insufferable prig."[2]

Getting over my self-righteousness means freedom from pretending I'm in control when I'm clearly not.

We'll never be lighthearted and childlike if we still think the answer is somehow "within ourselves." Little kids know they're dependent. It's obvious.

I tried to run away once in a huff, when I was six and we lived in Greenview, Illinois. I remember I was mad at my mom, so I packed a peanut butter sandwich and set off for the wide, wide world. I made it all the way to the lot across the street. Then I reconsidered and repented. It was kind of like the prodigal son story, except I was only gone for ten minutes.

My dependence chased me back to reality. It still does. This is why admitted addicts, or people who've hit rock bottom, have such an advantage over the rest of us.

This kind of dependence isn't weakness, by the way. It's strength. Acknowledging the reality of our dependence is not a weakness either. An astronaut on a spacewalk isn't "weak" for admitting he needs to be tethered to the station or needs a special suit for oxygen. It's obvious.

Dependence isn't weakness. The denial of our dependence is.

Getting over my self-righteousness means freedom from making an idiot of myself so often.

When I'm full of myself and my own supposed goodness, I talk too much. Maybe it's to subtly teach others a lesson I think they need, or maybe it's to overexplain my point of view so people will realize how correct I am. Or maybe it's to convince myself I'm right about something that I'm actually not qualified to even speak about. It could be just about anything, but it's all driven by me wanting me to be oh-so-right.

"You ever hear someone go on and on about something, and you realize they don't know what they're talking about? . . . God does this with Job and his friends," Anne Carlson

Kennedy writes. "Just lets them run off. He weighs in, and then you have to consider what to actually do about it. The correct response is to crumble to the ground. But that will change the way you see the world forever."[3]

Yes, the humbled life is very different. It can be hard. It's certainly counter to our instincts.

But one wonderful side effect involves me occasionally shutting up.

Getting over my self-righteousness means freedom to actually like people.

It's hard to genuinely like people if I'm judging them. If I have a contrite and broken spirit, I give up the judging altogether. This isn't moral relativism. *I don't cease judging people because I no longer believe in the idea of sin. I give up judging people because I believe in the reality of sin so fervently.* It's because I know sin's danger and deadliness firsthand. This is why one alcoholic can root so wholeheartedly for another.

For what it's worth, if you're interested in persuading people, this whole "liking them" concept is very effective. I've noticed people won't listen without it. They won't care about my insightful political opinions or my deeply held convictions.

> If you're interested in persuading people, this whole "liking them" concept is very effective.

Liking people isn't easy for some of us. Yes, I tend to prefer dogs to humans. I also tend to prefer robots to humans. And puppets. Perhaps you can relate. Nevertheless, I've found it much easier to like other people when I'm aware of my own need for God.

Getting over my self-righteousness means freedom to be more creative.

Humility means having far less to worry about. When you aren't so concerned about your reputation, you can be free to be more creative. The specter of failure isn't lurking behind every project.

As Thomas Merton wrote, "To penetrate the truth of how utterly unimportant we are is the only thing that can set us free to enjoy true happiness."[4] He's not saying we're "unimportant" to God, of course. We just realize that, in the scheme of things, this big thing I'm doing really isn't so big at all.

When I take myself too seriously, I get stressed about things that should be enjoyable. I love my radio job and I love public speaking, but I've noticed if I'm worried about myself and what others think of me, I get stressed about it and I do a poor job. If I start with a lighter heart and think, "What can I do to delight or encourage the people listening today?" it can be tremendously fun and the ideas flow.

Humility means you don't have to fear failure. There simply isn't so much at stake.

The other day my wife and daughter and I stood with a crowd in the sand. We were all focused on one particular individual named Teddy. Our attention was riveted on Teddy as he . . . did absolutely nothing.

Teddy is a sea turtle, and we were honestly confused by his lack of excitement. Years ago, he was injured but was nursed back to health at the local marine life center. He'd spent a very long time in a special tub of water, swimming in tight little circles. So this was his big day!

There had been an announcement online that Teddy was to be released back into the big, beautiful ocean. Everyone was amped. The beach was jammed. We all backed out of the way as four men lifted Teddy and placed him in front of the waves on the sand.

This is it! Here he goes!

. . . Except he didn't. He did nothing. Finally he looked at the blue water, looked at the horizon now open to him, and started to move . . . the other direction. He turned his massive turtle body around and started lumbering back to where he'd spent his captivity.

The four men ran out, picked him up again, turned him around, and set him down facing the ocean. They darted away as we all cheered Teddy on to sweet freedom! I got chills just knowing what a difference this would make in Teddy's life as he returned home.

He eyed the water and started to move again . . . the wrong direction. He wanted back in his water bin.

The four turtle carriers ran out again. They picked him up and turned him around. They set him down. He turned around again. They ran out, picked him up, set him down. . . . Same thing.

Then they picked him up again and this time carried him to the water line. They set him down, and as he started to turn around again, away from the ocean, a wave washed over him.

He froze.

He slowly turned back to look at the ocean. Another wave washed over him. And then he raised his head. And he started, ever so slowly, to move.

The crowd cheered.

Teddy picked up his pace. He was sure of himself now. He knew exactly what he wanted, and he threw himself into the water. We watched him until he was a speck in the big blue ocean, and then we could see him no more.

Teddy was off to the Gulf Stream, where he belonged.

So, yes, I'm Brant Hansen, and I'm not a good person.

I seem like a good guy, maybe, but you don't really know me. You don't know my thoughts. You don't know all my real motives, and you know what? Neither do I.

But I'm convinced the only one who really knows me loves me more than anyone else. More than I can imagine. It's a big relief.

> Show me your ways, Lord,
>   teach me your paths.
> Guide me in your truth and teach me,
>   for you are God my Savior,
>   and my hope is in you all day long. (Ps. 25:4–5)

His ways really are better. My way only leads back to captivity and excuse making. (Please don't sing "My Way" at my funeral. You're free to go with *The Muppet Show* theme.)

Jesus, the one who tells us repeatedly that we are not good, is the one who tells us his yoke is easy and his burden is light. It's taken me a while, but I'm convinced. This way really is easier, lighter, and simpler.

In the end, I think our autobiographies can be really short. We'll be able to sum up the entire story with a pause, maybe a laugh, and a simple, "I had my doubts, but you know what? God was good to me."

Acknowledgments

My first acknowledgment is that I'm a clumsy writer of acknowledgments. There are simply too many people to thank when it comes to writing a book like this. I depend on an extraordinary number of people to help me do things. (Have you heard of "executive function"? I don't have that.)

So I'll keep it short.

Thank you, editors at Baker Publishing Group. Thank you to my wonderful radio producer and ever-encouraging friend, Sherri Lynn. Thank you, listeners to our radio show and podcast. Thank you, Justice and Julia.

Mostly, though, I'm indebted to my wife, Carolyn. She breathes life into me.

I'd also like to acknowledge Kanye West; Stephen King; Tiger Woods; Jackie Chan; Robert Downey Jr.; Cristiano Ronaldo; Bono; J.Lo; Meghan, Duchess of Sussex; Steph Curry; and Dwayne "The Rock" Johnson. None of these people contributed to this *particular* book, but maybe someone will run across this book when they google the names of some celebrity people, and then they will have contributed in their own way, if you think about it.

Fun fact: I live (sort of) near Tiger Woods here in Florida. We don't hang out, but I do check the local Goodwill occasionally to see if he's dropped off any Nike stuff.

Notes

Chapter 1: Dear Everybody

1. Emma Young, "Belief in Our Moral Superiority Is the Most Irrational Self-Enhancing Bias of All," The British Psychological Society Research Digest, November 29, 2017, https://digest.bps.org.uk/2017/11/29/belief-in-our-moral-superiority-is-the-most-irrational-self-enhancing-bias-of-all.

2. Cindi May, "Most People Consider Themselves to Be Morally Superior," *Scientific American*, January 31, 2017, https://www.scientificamerican.com/article/most-people-consider-themselves-to-be-morally-superior.

3. Sarah Griffiths, "Prisoners Believe They Have Better Morals Than People on the Outside, Claims Study," Dailymail.com, January 9, 2014, https://www.dailymail.co.uk/sciencetech/article-2536459/Prisoners-believe-better-morals-people-outside-claims-study.html.

4. Renee Carr, quoted in Danielle Page, "What Happens to Your Brain When You Binge-Watch a TV Series," Nbcnews.com, November 4, 2017, https://www.nbcnews.com/better/health/what-happens-your-brain-when-you-binge-watch-tv-series-ncna816991.

5. W. H. Auden, *The Age of Anxiety: A Baroque Eclogue* (Princeton: Alan Jacobs, 1947), 105.

6. Steve Brown, "Self-Righteousness: The Secret to Getting Better," Keylife.org, July 12, 2017, https://www.keylife.org/articles/self-righteousness-the-secret-to-getting-better.

Chapter 2: Wronger Than We Think

1. Kathleen Schulz, *Being Wrong* (New York: HarperCollins, 2010), 4.

2. Schulz, 72–73.

3. Tom Vanderbilt, *Traffic* (New York: Alfred Knopf, 2008), 63–65.

4. Daniel Kahneman, quoted in Ben Yagoda, "Your Lying Mind: The Cognitive Biases Tricking Your Brain," *Atlantic*, September 2018, https://www.theatlantic.com/magazine/archive/2018/09/cognitive-bias/565775.

5. K. E. Stanovich, R. F. West, and M. E. Toplak, "Myside Bias, Rational Thinking, and Intelligence," *Current Directions in Psychological Science* 22, August 5, 2013, doi:10.1177/0963721413480174.

6. Herbert M. Jenkins and William C. Ward, "Judgment of Contingency between Responses and Outcomes," *American Psychological Association* 79 (1979): 1–17.

Chapter 3: Your Very Own PR Firm—and Why You Should Fire Them

1. R. E. Nisbett and T. D. Wilson, "Telling More Than We Can Know: Verbal Reports on Mental Processes," *Psychological Review* 84 (May 1977): 231–59.

2. Lauren Migliore, "The Neuroscience behind Rationalizing Our Mistakes," *Brain World*, May 2, 2018, https://brainworldmagazine.com/the-neuroscience-behind-rationalizing-our-mistakes/, italics mine.

3. Jonathan Haidt, *The Righteous Mind: Why Good People Are Divided by Politics and Religion* (New York: Vintage Books, 2012), 91–92.

Chapter 4: Aristotle and My Garage Sale

1. Daniel Kahneman, Jack L. Knetsch, and Richard H. Thaler, "Experimental Tests of the Endowment Effect and the Coase Theorem," *Journal of Political Economy* 98 (December 1990): 1325–48.

2. Jason F. Shogren, Seung Y. Shin, Dermot J. Hayes, and James B. Kliebenstein, "Resolving Differences in Willingness to Pay and Willingness to Accept," *American Economic Review* 84 (March 1994): 255–70.

3. Aristotle, *The Nicomachean Ethics*, trans. F. H. Peters (Altenmünster, Germany: Jazzybee Verlag, 1893), 153.

4. Jennifer Billock, "Why We Stalk Our Exes on Facebook," Mental floss.com, June 1, 2015, http://mentalfloss.com/article/64513/why-we-stalk-our-exes-facebook, italics mine.

5. John T. Jones, Brett W. Pelham, Mauricio Carvallo, and Matthew C. Mirenberg, "How Do I Love Thee? Let Me Count the Js: Implicit Egotism and Interpersonal Attraction," *Journal of Personality and Social Psychology* 87 (November 2004): 665–83.

6. Lindsay Dodgson, "It Turns Out Opposites Probably Don't Attract—Here's Why We Like People Who Are Similar to Ourselves,"

Businessinsider.com, March 11, 2018, https://www.businessinsider.com
/why-opposites-dont-attract-2018-3.

7. Ashley Killough, "Jeb Bush Questions Donald Trump's Faith,"
CNN.com, January 26, 2016, https://www.cnn.com/2016/01/26/politics
/jeb-bush-donald-trump-faith/index.html.

8. Michael Foust, "Obama: Sin Is What Doesn't Match My Values,"
Baptist Press, March 2, 2012, http://www.bpnews.net/37310/obama-sin
-is-what-doesnt-match-my-values.

Chapter 5: Follow Your Heart: The Worst Advice Ever

1. Thoughts of Dog (@dog_feelings), Twitter, January 27, 2018,
https://twitter.com/dog_feelings/status/957385573571944455?lang=en.

2. Michael Foley, *The Age of Absurdity: Why Modern Life Makes It
Hard to Be Happy* (London: Simon and Schuster, 2010), 53.

3. Haidt, *The Righteous Mind*, xxi.

4. Guy Swanson, *Ego Defenses and the Legitimization of Behavior*
(Cambridge: Cambridge University Press, 1988), 14.

5. Swanson, 26.

6. D. N. Perkins, M. Farady, and B. Bushey, "Everyday Reasoning and
the Roots of Intelligence," *Informal Reasoning and Education*, eds. J. F.
Voss, D. N. Perkins, and J. W. Segal (Hillsdale, NJ: Lawrence Erlbaum
Associates, Inc., 1991), 83–105.

7. Nicole Weinrauch, "Khmer Rouge Tribunal Ends with Justification,
Not Denial," *Cambodia Daily*, June 29, 2017, https://www.cambodiadaily
.com/news/khmer-rouge-tribunal-ends-denial-not-justification-131950.

8. Tomas Venclova, "The Prince and His Czar—Letters from Exile,"
New York Times, February 14, 1988, https://www.nytimes.com/1988/02
/14/books/the-prince-and-his-czar-letters-from-exile.html.

Chapter 6: The Flaw in Our Code

1. James Hibberd, "Westworld Co-Creator Defends Complex Plotting, Humanity Criticism," *Entertainment Weekly*, June 25, 2018, https://
ew.com/tv/2018/06/25/westworld-interview-nolan.

2. Jonathan Nolan, quoted in Hibberd.

3. Nathan W. Bingham, "The State of Theology: What Do People Really
Believe in 2018?," Ligonier Ministries, October 16, 2018, https://www
.ligonier.org/blog/state-theology-what-do-people-really-believe-2018.

4. R. Dale Guthrie, *The Nature of Paleolithic Art* (Chicago: University
of Chicago Press, 2005), 422.

5. Chris Hedges, "What Every Person Should Know about War," *New York Times*, July 6, 2003, https://www.nytimes.com/2003/07/06/books/chapters/what-every-person-should-know-about-war.html.

6. Adam Withnall, "World Peace? These Are the Only 11 Countries in the World That Are Actually Free from Conflict," *Independent*, August 14, 2014, https://www.independent.co.uk/news/world/politics/world-peace-these-are-the-only-11-countries-in-the-world-that-are-actually-free-from-conflict-9669623.html.

7. Paul Johnson, *Intellectuals* (New York: Harper and Row, 1988), 1–27.

8. Thomas Merton, quoted in Brennan Manning, *The Ragamuffin Gospel* (Colorado Springs: Multnomah, 2015), 11.

Chapter 7: Mixed Motives

1. John M. Darley and Daniel C. Batson, "From Jerusalem to Jericho: A Study of Situational and Dispositional Variables in Helping Behavior," *Journal of Personality and Social Psychology* 27 (1973): 100–108.

2. University of Cambridge, "Removing Sweets from Checkouts Linked to Dramatic Fall in Unhealthy Snack Purchases," Science Daily, December 18, 2018, https://www.sciencedaily.com/releases/2018/12/181218171553.htm.

3. Timothy Keller, *Encounters with Jesus* (New York: Penguin Books, 2016), 69.

4. Hannah Arendt, "Eichmann in Jerusalem—I," *New Yorker*, February 16, 1963, https://www.newyorker.com/magazine/1963/02/16/eichmann-in-jerusalem-i.

5. Henri Nouwen, *The Way of the Heart* (New York: Ballantine Books, 1991), 21.

Chapter 8: So Why Are We Like This?

1. Dallas Willard, quoted in John Ortberg, *Soul Keeping: Caring for the Most Important Part of You* (Grand Rapids: Zondervan, 2014), 155.

2. John Trent and Gary Smalley, *The Blessing: Giving the Gift of Unconditional Love and Acceptance* (Nashville: Thomas Nelson, 2011), 37.

3. Trent and Smalley, 133–45.

Chapter 9: Hide the Bud Light Towel: Adventures in Guilt

1. Flavia Dzodan, "Come One, Come All! Feminist and Social Justice Blogging as Performance and Bloodshed," Libcom.org, February 24,

2014, https://libcom.org/library/come-one-come-all-feminist-social-just ice-blogging-performance-bloodshed, italics mine.

2. Helen Andrews, "Shame Storm," *First Things*, January 2019, https:// www.firstthings.com/article/2019/01/shame-storm.

3. Will Campbell, *Brother to a Dragonfly* (Jackson, MS: University Press of Mississippi, 1977), 187.

Chapter 10: Let's Freak People Out

1. Ben Kaye, "John Lennon's Testy Post-Beatles Breakup Letter to Paul McCartney Shared Online," Consequenceofsound.net, November 15, 2016, https://consequenceofsound.net/2016/11/john-lennons-testy-post -beatles-breakup-letter-to-paul-mccartney-shared-online

2. Kaye.

3. Be Scofield, "Why the Dalai Lama Is Wrong to Think Meditation Will Eliminate Violence," *Tikkun Daily*, November 15, 2012, https:// www.tikkun.org/tikkundaily/2012/11/15/why-the-dalai-lama-is-wrong -to-think-meditation-will-eliminate-violence.

4. Caveat Magister, "This Is Not the Utopia You're Looking For," *Burning Man Journal*, October 10, 2017, https://journal.burningman.org /2017/10/opinion/serious-stuff/this-is-not-the-utopia-youre-looking-for.

Chapter 11: The Worst Wonderful Word

1. Luke Abrahams, "These Are the 'Most Hated' Words in the English Language," Culturetrip.com, February 7, 2018, https://theculturetrip.com /europe/articles/these-are-the-most-hated-words-in-the-english-language.

2. Wes Enzinna, "Renouncing Hate: What Happens When a White Nationalist Repents," *New York Times*, September 10, 2018, https:// www.nytimes.com/2018/09/10/books/review/eli-saslow-rising-out-of -hatred.html.

3. Betsy Bates Freed, "When Terminal Cancer Patients Don't Get the Message," Mdedge.com, November 2, 2012, https://www.mdedge.com /psychiatry/article/56581/pain/when-terminal-cancer-patients-dont -get-message.

4. Schulz, *Being Wrong*, 232–41.

5. Manning, *Ragamuffin Gospel*, 11.

Chapter 12: A Chainsaw at CVS

1. Steve Doughty, "Pop Goes the Funeral as Hymns Fade Out: Frank Sinatra's My Way Is Now Top Choice as Increasing Numbers Have a Play-list for Their Send-Off," Dailymail.com, August 31, 2016, https://www

.dailymail.co.uk/news/article-3766145/Pop-goes-funeral-hymns-fade
-Frank-Sinatra-s-Way-choice-increasing-numbers-playlist-send-off.html.

2. William Ernest Henley, "Invictus," *Book of Verses* (New York: Charles Scribner's Sons, 1893), 56.

3. Hannah Arendt, "Eichmann in Jerusalem—I."

4. George MacDonald, quoted in C. S. Lewis, *George MacDonald, An Anthology: 365 Readings* (New York: HarperCollins, 1973), 103.

Chapter 13: Seven Billion Italian Stallions

1. Aleksandr Solzhenitsyn, *The Gulag Archipelago: An Experiment in Literary Investigation*, trans. Thomas P. Whitney and Harry Willets, abr. Edward E. Ericson Jr. (New York: HarperCollins, 1976), 75.

2. Swanson, *Ego Defenses*, 159.

3. Nick Chester, "Criminals Explain How They Justified Their Crimes to Themselves," Vice.com, April 21, 2016, https://www.vice.com/en_us /article/gqmz4m/how-criminals-justify-crimes-psychology-gangsters-uk.

4. Chester.

5. Chester.

6. Joe Rogan, "Joe Rogan Experience #880: Jon Jones," December 1, 2016, https://www.youtube.com/watch?v=cBSwJnZpUI8.

Chapter 14: A Short Chapter about the Previous Chapter

1. Dallas Willard, *The Divine Conspiracy: Rediscovering Our Hidden Life in God* (New York: HarperCollins, 1998), 149.

2. Mark Helprin, *A Soldier of the Great War* (San Diego: Harcourt Brace & Company, 1991), 454.

3. Ortberg, *Soul Keeping*, 72.

Chapter 15: How to Get Kicked Out of the Church of Satan

1. David Foster Wallace, "David Foster Wallace on Life and Work," *Wall Street Journal*, September 19, 2008, https://www.wsj.com/articles /SB122178211966454607.

2. Rick Warren, *The Purpose Driven Life* (Grand Rapids: Zondervan, 2012), 262.

3. M. Mandrake, "On the Definition of Satanism," Churchofsatan.com, accessed August 13, 2019, https://www.churchofsatan.com/on-definition -of-satanism.

4. Preston Sprinkle, "Love Your . . . Enemies?" Prestonsprinkle.com, August 31, 2016, https://www.prestonsprinkle.com/blog/2016/8/31/love -yourenemies?rq=love%20your%20enemies.

5. Michael H. Hart, *The 100: A Ranking of the Most Influential Persons in History* (New York: Kensington Publishing Corp., 1992), vii.

Chapter 16: Even More Good News: The Humble Life Is More Fun Anyway

1. Wallace, "David Foster Wallace on Life and Work."
2. Amor Towles, *A Gentleman in Moscow* (New York: Penguin, 2016), 196.

Chapter 17: The Final Chapter: The One Where I Finally Mention Kermit

1. Henri Nouwen, *Here and Now: Living in the Spirit* (New York: Crossroad Publishing, 1994), 117.
2. N. T. Wright, *After You Believe: Why Christian Character Matters* (New York: HarperCollins, 2010), 61.
3. Anne Kennedy, *Nailed It: 365 Sarcastic Devotions for Angry or Worn-Out People* (Oro Valley, AZ: Kalos Press, 2016), 174.
4. Thomas Merton, *The Sign of Jonas* (San Diego: Harcourt, 1979), 273.

Brant Hansen is an author, nationally syndicated radio host, and advocate for healing children with correctible disabilities through CURE International. His podcast with his friend and radio producer, *The Brant and Sherri Oddcast*, has been downloaded millions of times. The author of *Unoffendable* and *Blessed Are the Misfits*, Hansen has written for CNN .com, the *Washington Post*, *U.S. News and World Report*, the *South Florida Sun Sentinel*, *Relevant*, and numerous other outlets on matters as varied as public policy, culture, sports, Asperger's syndrome, and faith. He and his wife, Carolyn, live in South Florida.

Connect with
BRANT

Visit **BRANTHANSEN.COM**
for Brant's radio show, blog, podcast, and more!

 BrantHansen    BrantHansenPage

Thank you for reading this book.

I want to leave you with a challenge (and if you can't do it or don't want to do it, that's okay).

Here it is: *Help us heal kids and tell them and their families how much they are loved by God.*

There are millions of kids with disabilities that are correctable. They're subject to abuse and intense rejection. They're often considered cursed. But getting access to surgery changes everything for them.

That's what CURE does! This has been my passion for years. I've visited these hospitals and met these kids, these families, these doctors . . . and this looks like Jesus to me.

Kids can walk and skip and dance and run for the first time in their lives! Moms and dads are crying with joy!

This is what I wish we followers of Jesus were known for: healing. **Please consider jumping online right now (**cure.org**) and becoming a CURE Hero.**

And if you want some amazing inspiration (and to see where your money is going!), check out this documentary on Amazon Prime or YouTube.

cure

WINNER
BEST CINEMATOGRAPHY DOCUMENTARY
GREAT LAKES CHRISTIAN
FILM FESTIVAL
2018

NOMINEE
MOST INSPIRATIONAL DOCUMENTARY
INTERNATIONAL CHRISTIAN
FILM FESTIVAL
2018

WINNER
MOST INSPIRATIONAL AWARD
CHRISTIAN WORLDVIEW
FILM FESTIVAL
2018

CURE INTERNATIONAL PRESENTS

MODERN DAY
MIRACLES